www.colour

FF 00 00
00 FF 00
00 00 FF

www.colour

ROGER PRING

SERIES CONSULTANT
ALASTAIR CAMPBELL

CASSELL
ILLUSTRATED

To Sarah, Sally and Katy

First published in the United Kingdom in 2000 by Cassell & Co

Copyright © 2000 The Ilex Press Limited

This revised edition first published in 2003

For more information on this title and others in the series, please visit: www.designdirectories.com

Trademarks and trademark names are used throughout this book to describe and inform you about various proprietary products. Such mention is intended to benefit the owner of the trademark and is not intended to infringe copyright nor to imply any claim to the mark other than that made by its owner.

The information contained in this book is given without warranty and, while every precaution has been taken in compiling the book, neither the author nor publisher assume any responsibility or liability whatsoever to any person or entity with respect to any errors which may exist in the book, nor for any loss of data which may occur as the result of such errors or for the efficacy or performance of any product or process described in the book.

A CIP catalogue record for this book is available from the British Library

ISBN 1 84403 107 1

This book was conceived, designed and produced by The Ilex Press Limited The Barn, College Farm 1 West End, Whittlesford Cambridge CB2 4LX

Sales Office:
The Old Candlemakers West Street, Lewes East Sussex BN7 2NZ

Editorial Director:
Sophie Collins
Art Director:
Alastair Campbell
Managing Editor:
Shuet-Kei Cheung
Editor:
Peter Leek
Additional material:
Howard Oakley
Web research:
Graham Davis
Designers:
Graham Davis and Roger Pring.
Illustrations:
John Woodcock and Alastair Campbell.

Originated and printed by Hong Kong Graphic, Hong Kong

Cassell Illustrated 2–4 Heron Quays London E14 4JP

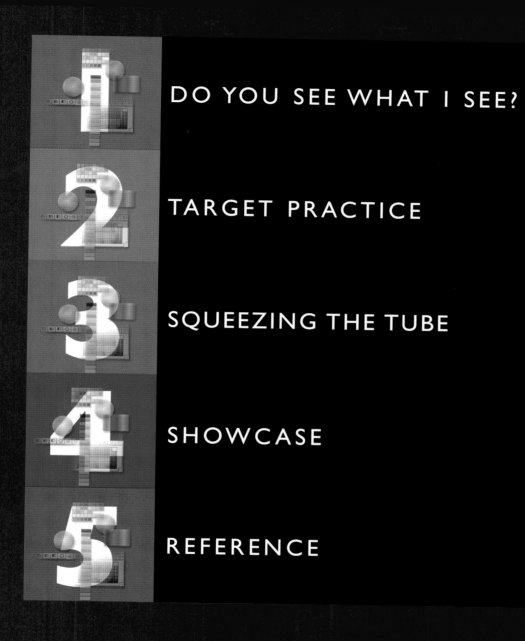

INTRODUCTION

Colour is painless and very nearly automatic. On screen, you can use any colour you like, including many that you never see in nature. You can create landscapes of cinematic complexity and splendour; sweeping gradients of brilliant hues, jewel-studded and intersected by glowing shafts of light; cornucopias of intensely desirable images displayed against infinite vistas of total chromatic perfection. You can see them, even now, in your mind's eye, detailed and gleaming. Can your vision be shared?

Colour on the Web is complex and needs careful management. On screen, you are likely to be limited to an apparently arbitrary palette that includes colours you may wish never to see again. Your theatre of action is limited to a little window the size and quality of which is not yours to control, and within which anarchy may arise without notice. So, your glistening canvas must be taken down from the studio wall, sliced into tiny fragments, rolled up tightly and inserted into a thin and capricious pipe for delivery to its audience. Despite all this, your vision can be shared; the colourfully seductive brilliance and saturation of the screen will conspire to make it memorable. Green for go.

Roger Pring

London

SEEING RED

Red doesn't exist; neither does Pantone® 485, nor flame-cherry vermilion gloss. The only real red is FF0000. Try this simple test to prove it – take a strawberry, a colour-sample book, a lipstick and a colour monitor showing full-value red; put them in a room from which all light has been excluded, and observe.

The only red you see is on the screen. Electrons from the gun at the back of the tube bombard the screen phosphors and selectively excite the red ones. They glow, and you see red. Close your eyes, and pretty soon the equivalent shape in blue will appear on the inside of your eyelids. If you're later asked to describe the red you saw, you can recall its intensity but you can't describe the experience by reference to any other kind of redness. This red is unique to the screen – more intense than fruit, more memorable than a sample chip of colour, and more seductive than lipstick.

The blue after-image signals that the inside of your eyes has been affected, though only temporarily, by this experience of red. Moreover, you may have undergone a subtle change of mood in a subliminal reaction to this chromatic exposure. An increased heart rate and a heightened predisposition to aggression or lust may ensue – so be careful when observing the test block (*above right*).

Concentrate hard on the black disc (*top*) for 15 seconds, then stare at the lower disc for a further 15. One of the sensitive chemicals (rhodopsin) in the cones of your retina will become temporarily bleached by exposure to red, and will interpret the white paper as a bright turquoise.

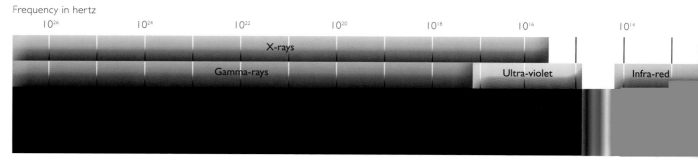

Frequency in hertz

| 10^{26} | 10^{24} | 10^{22} | 10^{20} | 10^{18} | 10^{16} | 10^{14} |

X-rays

Gamma-rays

Ultra-violet

Infra-red

What is light made of?

Isaac Newton (1642–1727) used a glass prism to demonstrate that 'white light' was actually composed of a range of spectral colours.

Through a tiny hole, he let a beam of sunlight into a completely dark chamber. Striking the prism, the light separated out fanwise into its constituent colours – from red at one end to violet at the other. Using a second prism, he was able to recombine the coloured rays into white light. His assistant, possessing better colour vision than his master, was able to discern seven colours: red, orange, yellow, green, blue, indigo and violet.

Having seen how colours could be refracted, Newton went on to explain the means by which objects appeared 'coloured', using his theory of 'corpuscles'. He believed that all objects were covered with a microscopically thin layer of

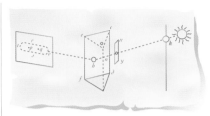

refracting cells, whose differing sizes determined the objects' apparent colour when irradiated with a continuous stream of light.

A hundred years later, Thomas Young discovered that light is not a stream of particles, but is made of a succession of waves. It is the size of these waves that determines their colour.

At the end of the 19th century, James Clerk Maxwell went on to show that visible light forms only a small section of the electromagnetic spectrum. Colours could now be precisely described in terms of their wavelength.

3

Carrots, not surprisingly, contain a heavy dose of carotenoids. These pigments absorb shorter-wavelength (blue) light and reflect the longer (red/orange/yellow) frequencies.

3

11

| 10^{10} | 10^{8} | 10^{6} | **2** |

Radio waves

Microwaves

2

The electromagnetic spectrum (*left*) runs from radio waves that are several hundred metres long to very short (high-frequency) X-rays and gamma rays. Visible rays are in a tiny range, from 400 nanometres (blue) to 700nm (red.)

AN EXPOSED PIECE OF THE BRAIN

In the competitive waters of the primordial swamp, organisms appeared whose brains had evolved to the point where external 'buds' formed outside the brain case.

This apparently grisly development was the first stage in the formation of the human eye, and also accounts for the curious fact that the light-sensitive layers of the eye appear to be 'inside out' from an engineering point of view. Light has to penetrate a layer of cells, which reduce its intensity before it strikes the vital receptors. This is also the cause of the receptor-less 'blind spot', where the optic nerve has to make its necessary exit from the orb of the eye on its way to the brain.

The ancient wisdom of Euclid (c. 300 BC) was that the eye itself sprayed the passing scene with a stream of mysterious light, and coloured objects achieved a temporary existence. The reality is exactly opposite, as we now smugly know. The red part of this strawberry has absorbed all other colours of the visible spectrum and radiates back only strawberry red. Even these rays are not coloured in the ordinary sense: they are just waves vibrating at the frequency of red light.

Finally, the eye focuses these waves on the retina, and the 'red' rays excite tiny receptors especially sensitive to that wavelength. Nearby receptors react to 'blue' and 'green' rays, so the yellow pips on the strawberry's surface activate the green receptors also (yellow in these terms is red plus green), while the leaf is 'seen' by the green receptor only. The resulting electrical activity sends signals along the optic nerve to the brain. Along this pathway the image is turned 'right side up', and arrives in the lower part of the left hemisphere of the brain – which is where colour finally arises. About 30% of all the grey matter in the brain is concerned with image processing, while unknown millions of neural links deal with the tricky matter of choosing a 'nice' colour.

12

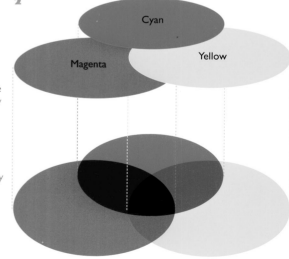

1 | 2
The additive system (*left*) is the basis of colour management on screen. The three converging red, blue and green lights produce white where they overlap; the only surprising result is the yellow made by red and green. The mixtures in the subtractive system (*right*) seems intuitively more familiar. These three colours plus a reinforcing black are the stuff of conventional paper printing.

1

2

Cyan

Yellow

Magenta

How does the brain see?

Sitting at a computer screen, you might imagine the eye/brain combination to resemble a rather elaborate flat-bed scanner. The scanner, having recorded the image in successive passes, presents it to the computer as a stream of data that can be displayed on the screen, processed and stored on a hard disk. Each bit of data has exactly the same status as its companions, and its electrical pulse is interpreted uniformly as part of the whole picture.

This analogy is entirely wrong. The part of the brain that handles visual stimuli operates on many more levels. The diagram shows the location of the processing areas. Some of their functions are understood; and some are effectively colour-blind, dealing only with movement or dark/light boundaries. One section of the brain deals exclusively with colour, and there is a smaller section that responds to colour when defined by shape.

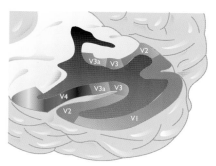

The back of the brain (*left*), with the 'vision' areas of the left hemisphere. V1 deals with broad areas of depth and motion; the superior temporal sulcus processes motion only. V2, V3 and V3a are for edges, depth and defined areas of colour; V4 handles colour only.

3

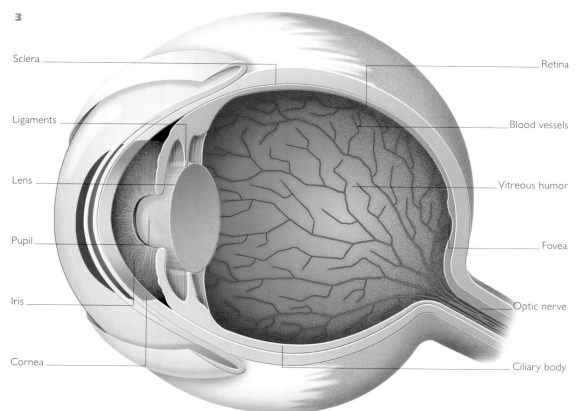

Sclera
Ligaments
Lens
Pupil
Iris
Cornea

Retina
Blood vessels
Vitreous humor
Fovea
Optic nerve
Ciliary body

3

The human eye is an extraordinarily complex structure. At the front it has an elegant windscreen equipped with a wiping system fed by a continuous stream of cleaning fluid; the centre has a pressurized clear jelly that helps maintain the shape of the orb; at the back is a chemical film of electrically connected sensors which connect to the brain via a fine cable. In addition there is auto-focus, auto-exposure and low-light capability. But no zoom, so far.

KEEPING IT REAL

Kwas for black. C was for cyan, M for magenta and Y for yellow. So far so obvious (though K in fact stood for 'key plate', since B could equally well have signified black or blue). These colours formed the pillars of print, and the inadvertent inclusion of RGB elements in a print job was as popular as coughing at a concert.

Now, in the purely electronic environment of the Internet, the old four-colour set is equally unwelcome. In fact, the screen image routinely attains a higher range of colour, contrast and saturation than any kind of paper-based process. Naturally, there is a crossover where print-based designs need to be remanufactured for the screen, but there is no such constraining legacy for new design.

So, what could be better? A palette of brilliant saturated colour with the ability to represent a wide contrast range, instant feedback and correction on screen, animation, sound, a global audience absolutely at home with the televisual image – surely, all is for the best in this best of all possible worlds? The gap in this apparently seamless scenario is the pinhead-sized blot on the landscape called bandwidth. Using a simple wired network, the desktop computer can transmit hundreds of megabytes of data in very short order. The creaking telephone lines that now form the last link in the Internet delivery chain are very slow by comparison, easily overwhelmed by peaks in demand and choking over relatively tiny file sizes. Though a picture may paint a thousand words, in this environment words are more economical. To be precise, a thousand e-mail words would occupy 8k and an average 300-pixel-square RGB screen reproduction of the Mona Lisa uses up 264k.

14

Time to go home? The old rosettes of the conventional four-colour process (*left*). The enlarged section is magnified 1,300%. Compare these dots with those opposite.

2 | 3 | 4
A transparency
with a wide contrast
range – shown first
in four-colour print
(2), then as a JPEG
on an 8-bit screen
(256 colours) (3),
and finally on a 24-bit
monitor (millions of
colours) (4).

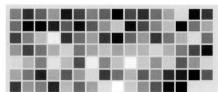

5
Reducing the same
image (*far left*) to
indexed colour shows
the effect of dithering.
The choice of 'exact
palette' during the
indexing process
results in a palette of
110 colours (*above*),
enough to preserve
the overall appear-
ance. The magnified
version shows the
pixel structure for
comparison only
(there is no magnifi-
cation on the Net).

MONITORING PROGRESS

In a conventional CRT (cathode-ray tube) monitor the screen image is made of glowing phosphors – organic chemicals that degrade progressively over time. A precisely repeating pattern (the 'trio') of red, green and blue dots is applied to the inside face of the screen, with a matching mask slightly to the rear. The electron guns at the rear of the tube activate each phosphor dot selectively as they sweep across the screen. There are two principal mask types: aperture grille and shadow mask (*see right*). This technology is at a mature stage of development, with a range of flat, or nearly flat, screens on offer. Extraordinary efforts, both optical and electronic, have produced monitors that occupy half the desk space of their ancestors – but the battle appears to be lost, the CRT is under attack from devices that dispense with its bulky glass tube and fearsome voltages.

The demand for laptops forced the pace of development of the current crop of LCD (liquid-crystal display) monitors. The properties of these crystals have been known for many years, but there is a great technical gulf between the familiar LCD calculator display panel and the multi-layered structure of a colour monitor. In the former, colours are produced by selectively activating each of the minuscule transistors at the rearmost level of the back-lit screen. Each transistor is equivalent to a pixel, capped with a red, green or blue filter, and the light output of the pixel is controlled by varying the voltage applied to the polarized panels that form the upper layers of the screen. A medium-size LCD monitor may contain a total of over two million such RGB pixels. In spite of the extreme rigour of the production process, many screens contain a tiny proportion of faulty pixels; either 'dead' or permanently 'lit'. One screen manufacturer opines that 20 of these inactive pixels (0.0008%) per screen constitutes an acceptable fault level. If possible, check your chosen screen before buying. Dead pixels can never be resurrected.

Further developments are afoot with FED (Field Emission Display), otherwise known as PDP (Plasma Display Panels). Currently these are employed for large-scale display, but monitor-size versions will arrive before long. The design is an elegant synthesis of CRT and LCD principles, but the reliance on phosphors currently means that such displays have a limited life.

1

The shadow-mask grille (*right*) is shown much magnified. The mask's purpose is to ensure that the beam is accurately directed on to the relevant phosphor.

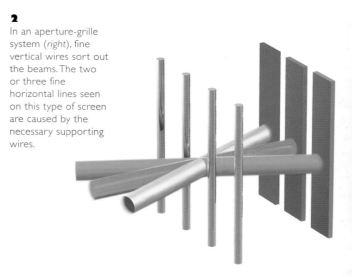

2

In an aperture-grille system (*right*), fine vertical wires sort out the beams. The two or three fine horizontal lines seen on this type of screen are caused by the necessary supporting wires.

3 640 x 480 pixels

4 832 x 624

5 1024 x 768

6 640 x 480

7 800 x 600

8 1152 x 864

3 | 4 | 5 | 6 | 7 | 8
Most monitors have switchable resolutions. The Macintosh examples (3, 4, 5) show the most usual settings. The PC screens (6, 7, 8) fall in a similar range. HTML text formatted on a Mac screen looks bigger on a PC; the converse is true in the other direction.

17

LOST IN SPACE

There have been numerous attempts to formalize the description of colour, resulting in a variety of competing standards. This is an area with a long history, and even longer shelves in technical libraries. The literature is concerned with dyestuffs, paint pigments and printing inks, and the aim has been to create a standard that enables colours to be named, defined in mathematical terms, and reproduced accurately time after time.

When colour arrived on computer monitors, there was no pressing need to define a standard for controlling the relationship between the screen image and the printed output. In those prehistoric times there was a meagre spectrum containing eight colours – including black and white – and primitive printers struggled to output the results in shades of grey.

Fast forward through the last two decades of the 20th century to the present day. Nowadays even an average screen can show 'millions of colours', while printers routinely interpret that screen image in 'photographically real' terms. The demand for repeatability across a range

of devices is irresistible, driven by graphic-arts users who expect fidelity between their screens and the printed image. This is a hard row to hoe – between the multiplicity of software interests, the myriad technologies for delivering ink to paper and the end user's capacity to administer a workable regime. Everyone has admirable intentions, but it's difficult to navigate through the marketplace to the holy grail of a solid system that will not cause more trouble than it cures.

The Web designer, though, may affect to scorn this turmoil. After all, how can you go wrong with only 216 colours, many of which appear to be the same? If you design Web pages solely for your own offline consumption and never include elements that will have a printed existence elsewhere, possess a monitor that never wanders from a true colour standard, never contemplate the possibility that the viewer might like to print your screen images in colour and believe that we shall be forever shackled by the 'Web-safe' cube, then scorn away. The rest of us need to pay attention.

1 | 2 | 3 | 4

In the l*a*b* colour space (see *page 19*), the full-colour image (*1*) is expressed as three sets of values (or channels). The first in the sequence (*2*) has values for image brightness; the second (*3*) for values on the green/red scale; and the third (*4*) those for blue/yellow. In actual practice, only the first, light/dark, channel is useful for image manipulation. The other two are too counter-intuitive for anything other than accidental effects.

The beginnings of colour standardization

The Commission Internationale d'Eclairage (CIE) defined a colour system in the early 1930s that enclosed all the colours a normal human eye could perceive. The CIE 'l*a*b*' space (right) is familiar in the Photoshop colour environment (below), though Photoshop dispenses with the asterisks. 'L' denotes the colour value on a light/dark scale; 'a' its position along the green/red axis; and 'b' its position along the blue/yellow axis. Unlike the RGB and CMYK spaces, l*a*b* does not depend on measurements particular to any input or output device. This 'device independence' makes it the preferred basis for producing

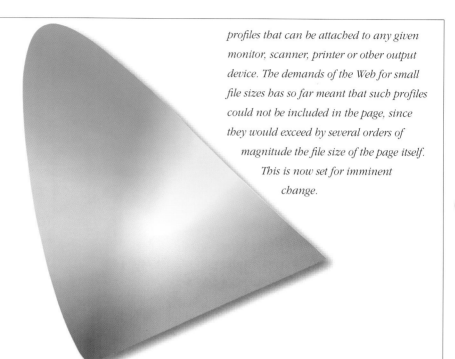

profiles that can be attached to any given monitor, scanner, printer or other output device. The demands of the Web for small file sizes has so far meant that such profiles could not be included in the page, since they would exceed by several orders of magnitude the file size of the page itself. This is now set for imminent change.

2
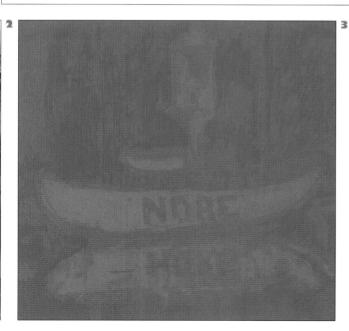

3

4

BIT BY BIT

The full point (full stop/period) at the end of this sentence is about 0.3mm tall, slightly larger than one pixel on a typical colour monitor. Though it may appear rather humble, such a pinprick is the end product of a considerable computing process. On a conventional CRT screen it is composed in its turn of three smaller phosphor dots, whose levels of red, green and blue determine its overall value. This tiny trio, mingling with its neighbours, gives the illusion of colour. If each of the three dots can be controlled to produce any one of 256 levels of intensity, you have 'millions of colours' (actually over 16 million (2^{24}) colours). In this 24-bit paradise, most colours of the visible spectrum can be shown or closely approximated. In the gloomier reaches of the real world, display inadequacies and lack of transmission bandwidth restrict the available palette to an 8-bit limbo; in this environment each pixel can only produce 256 different colours, though those 256 colours can be selected from a much wider palette (or colour look-up table/CLUT).

20

1 | 2 | 3 | 4
The ubiquitous chameleon suffers in the cause of art. The 1-bit or 'bitmap' image (1) is familiar from the candlelit era of screen imagery, while the 4-bit (16 colours) image (2) recalls slightly more recent machinery. 8-bit (3) delivers 256 colours and is the usual default for legions of domestic monitors. With 24 bits available (4) a full range of colours can be shown.

5 | 6 | 7
Temporarily restored to a less hysterical condition, the patient lizard is displayed for the record in 24-bit colour (5) with a rendition of the relevant 'millions of colours' space alongside. Comparison between the 'Web-safe' palette of 216 colours (6) and the adaptive palette (7), set to 256 colours, shows that there are losses of fidelity in the former, especially in adjoining areas of similar colour.

IN THE BLACK

Total colour-blindness is highly unusual. However, colour confusion is widespread. It seems that about 10% of the male population suffer to some degree from protanopia (red-green confusion), though it's uncommon in women. It may also entail confusion between red and grey. Less common is inability to distinguish between green and orange; or confusion between blue and green, or between green and blue/grey.

These misapprehensions are physiological in origin. Much more interesting are the preconceptions that the eye – or rather, the brain – applies to the surrounding world. Studies by Edwin Land, inventor of the Polaroid instant-picture system, show that the brain has a great

capacity to interpret, or even to fabricate, colour where none exists. In his experiments, a still life containing a variety of differently coloured and shaped objects was photographed with positive black-and-white film only, first through a yellow filter and subsequently through an orange one. The resulting transparencies, utterly devoid of colour, were then projected onto a screen through the same filters. As long as the pictures remained side by side, the audience could clearly see a strongly yellow monochromatic image alongside a largely similar orange version. With the projectors repositioned to superimpose the images exactly, almost all the colours of the original scene were suddenly re-created.

The implication is inescapable: though the eye may be a camera, the brain is more than just a roll of film. It responds to the difference in wavelengths and patterns of light between the two images, and makes educated guesses at the colours of familiar objects. At a lower level, the brain will see an apparently white surface as white, even though it may be illuminated with a very yellow tungsten lamp. This perceived 'white point' is crucial to all calibration procedures.

The 'whiteness' of the blank lit screen is formalized in three standards. After all, it would be fruitless to struggle to calibrate an image that was to be viewed alternately on a screen in a sunlit room, a fluorescently bright office and a dimly-lit garret. The principal standards are: D50 (warm yellow light at 5,000°K (degrees Kelvin)); D65 (6,500°K, which is equivalent to midday sunlight); and 9300 (9,300°K for cooler daylight). However, these are counsels of perfection, since you are unlikely to have control over the eventual viewing conditions of the image.

www.vischeck.com (*left*) is where you can take a very informal test of your colour vision.

Proper colour testing is more demanding, and needs to be done by a qualified optometrist.

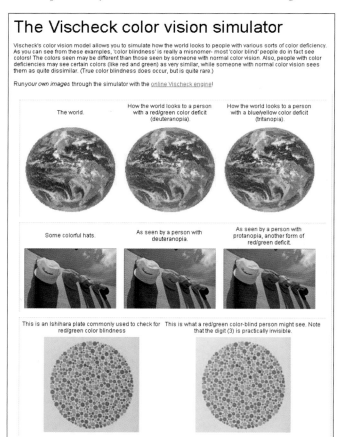

The Vischeck color vision simulator

Vischeck's color vision model allows you to simulate how the world looks to people with various sorts of color deficiency. As you can see from these examples, 'color blindness' is really a misnomer- most 'color blind' people do in fact see colors! The colors seen may be different than those seen by someone with normal color vision. Also, people with color deficiencies may see certain colors (like red and green) as very similar, while someone with normal color vision sees them as quite dissimilar. (True color blindness does occur, but is quite rare.)

Run *your own images* through the simulator with the online Vischeck engine!

The world.

How the world looks to a person with a red/green color deficit (deuteranopia).

How the world looks to a person with a blue/yellow color deficit (tritanopia).

Some colorful hats.

As seen by a person with deuteranopia.

As seen by a person with protanopia, another form of red/green deficit.

This is an Ishihara plate commonly used to check for red/green color blindness

This is what a red/green color-blind person might see. Note that the digit (3) is practically invisible.

The gamma question

There is a large obstacle to cross-platform screen harmony between Macs and PCs. Gamma is the measure of contrast displayed by a monitor, and traditionally it has been set at 1.8 for Apple Macintosh systems and 2.2 for PCs. The former has become the convention for print-based work, and the latter for the production of screen images. The example below shows uncorrected transfer between the two systems. Where gamma relates to colour space, the higher (PC) value has the inherent property of showing more shadow detail in any given image. It is therefore important that images processed in one gamma environment are converted correctly whenever they are transferred to another.

I These screen images (*left*) give an approximation of the colour cast differences between D50 (*1*), D65 (*2*) and 9300 (*3*).

Mac → PC

Mac ← PC

FINGER ON THE BUTTON

The routines outlined here are for the diligent. The hardware can be complex and some of the procedures tedious in the extreme, but the reward is a strikingly beautiful profile. The unifying purpose is to harmonize colour input and output across all devices. Grounded in the early work of the CIE, it gathers all the characteristics of a given machine into one portable file.

The International Consortium on Colour (ICC), founded in 1993, is a group of interested parties that administers ColorSync (for the Apple system) and the ICM standard (for Windows). Visit their Web site at **www.color.org** for a taste of the complexities behind the façade. The system depends also on the cooperation of device manufacturers in making available ready-made profiles to match each of their products.

This is an essentially reductive process. Anyone who has struggled with malfunctioning computer systems has already gained the costly wisdom that juggling variables in parallel is a recipe for premature ageing and hair loss. What's required is a rock-face with immovable pitons,

interlinked by taut ropes and leading to a brightly and truly coloured summit. Profiles are the trusty handholds in this ascent; and if the device manufacturer can't or won't provide them, you must make your own. There are several competing software solutions (the procedures shown opposite are based on the ColorBlind Matchbox system). For the ultimate in accuracy, the essentials are a spectrophotometer and a certain amount of obsessive behaviour. If you have less time, adequate colour vision and a smaller wallet, a good approximation can be obtained just by looking.

There is an evangelical aspect to these endeavours. In the age of Man's chromatic innocence there was no need for colour matching, and therefore no disagreement. As more devices come to the market, more contradictory voices are raised, more bizarre colour-delivery systems compete for attention, and false prophets may be heard in the land. The ICC, however, appears to have staked out the moral high ground; let us hope that, under their guidance, all our screens will one day shine equally with the true light.

ColorSync/ICM and sRGB

There is a struggle in prospect between the ICC profiles system and the sRGB colour space promoted by Microsoft and Hewlett-Packard. Whereas ColorSync/ICM attempts to deal with the whole supply chain from scanner and camera, through the 'creative' software package, to eventual screen or print output, sRGB is at present concerned solely with the relationship between the software and the receiving monitor. The sRGB specification, if adopted by all manufacturers, would mean common

qualities across all displays (the standard inevitably is based on Windows norms). It deals only with the average qualities of each device.

The most immediate effect of sRGB is for users of Photoshop, where the recent releases have sRGB as the default colour space. Files created in colour spaces other than sRGB (almost all for the immediate future) will open with a request for a conversion decision. Choosing 'convert' may lead to a gross change in the overall colour balance. Opinions differ as to the

safest course of action; in the absence of an accurate printed confirmation of the original colours, it may be prudent to refuse conversion and employ intuition instead. Alternatively, change the default colour space to one with which you are more confident.

Getting the colour right

On an adjustable monitor there are several routes to fine-tuning the screen image. Even the most basic display, with no apparent external controls, should be capable of adjustment by the system software. The user will see a sequence of test targets and can intuitively adjust the image for contrast and colour balance. Part of the typical Macintosh calibration

sequence is shown here (below left).

With the PANTONE Personal Calibrator, this operation is taken one stage further, using a thin plastic matrix applied to the screen surface. With this system, exact allowance can be made for the lighting conditions around the monitor. The end product is an ICC-compatible profile.

The basic ColorBlind Matchbox system employs a detector with rubber suction feet. While attached to the screen, it computes the actual output of the RGB guns. It also allows for the ambient lighting conditions and produces an ICC profile.

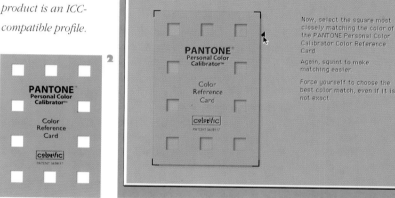

1
The Macintosh Monitor Calibration Assistant (*above*) leads the user through a set of fairly intuitive tests. This screen is the hardest of the five-screen sequence, requiring considerable squinting, blurring of vision and twisting in the chair to

establish the point at which the ubiquitous logotype merges most completely with its background. The built-in monitor profiles cover a wide range of devices.

2 | 3
The PANTONE Personal Calibrator displays a series of coloured squares, produced by each of the RGB guns. You set the colour balance by judging the point at which

the relevant colour seems about to fade. Finally, you apply the blue-plastic matrix

(*2*) to the screen, adjust the lighting to normal working conditions, and

attempt to match the perceived screen colour to the actual colour of the matrix.

4 | 5 | 6
The ColorBlind Matchbox system uses a miniature spectrophotometer (*below far left*), which is applied to the screen (*left*). A read-out of the signal from each of the guns is graphically displayed (*below left*) and can be corrected on screen.

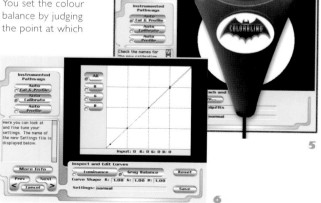

THE FURTHER PURSUIT OF PERFECTION

Delivery of accurate screen colour is only part of the picture. Your ideal viewer may want to print out your page as a record, a souvenir, of a joyful chromatic experience. Others may simply want a quick (and possibly dirty) black-and-white print for information only. In the latter case, your artfully contrived rainbow background and meaningfully coloured hierarchy of type is likely to dissolve into a morass of grey and similar dots. Sidestep this potential porridge by trying it for yourself as your page becomes more complex, or take a screen grab and check it out in a desaturated version.

The ideal viewer may use a less-than-ideal colour inkjet printer, with a life-expired ink cartridge printing on highly unsuitable paper. There is no known cure for this disorder. Your page should be prepared, however, with the virtuous assumption that all this will one day change for the better. Spectrophotometer calibration systems like the one shown here are currently very costly; they are designed to close the loop between the screen and a variety of input and output devices. Fortunately some of their functions can be approximated by trial and error.

1 | 2
A dedicated colour picker, like the one supplied by PANTONE (1) can be used within an image-editing or Web-page creation application to standardize Web-safe colour between screen and print. The accompanying swatch book (2) also gives the colour breakdown in RGB, CMYK, HTML and Hexachrome.

3
The traditional print-based PANTONE system also appears in the form of a colour picker (3) and swatch book. By definition, this is not a Web-safe environment – but for those working with the luxury of a 24-bit corporate intranet, for example, the business of matching corporate colours is made very straightforward.

4
Sophisticated devices like the MatchBox ColorBlind spectro-photometer show how things could be in the best of all possible worlds. Having calibrated the monitor with the companion screen photometer (see page 25), a test print can be made from one of a series of built-in colour test charts. In this case, a middle-of-the-road colour inkjet printer is being calibrated. The resulting print is then measured square by square, following a series of prompts from the software. This rather tedious process is worth it for the true perfectionist – the result is a profile that precisely reflects the qualities of the actual device being used. Regular recalibration will take care of any changes in ink colour or density. The test print can also be scanned or photo-graphed, or output to film to provide profiles for a range of input and output devices.

26

5

On the Web itself there are many sites offering help with calibration. At the sophisticated end of the spectrum, DisplayMate offer a commercial service for the video, film and TV industries. From **www.displaymate .com**, Windows users can download a series of free charts like the one below. The Turkish Photography Circle (*right*) help out, too, with monochrome and colour charts, and a challenging text workout for your eyeballs.

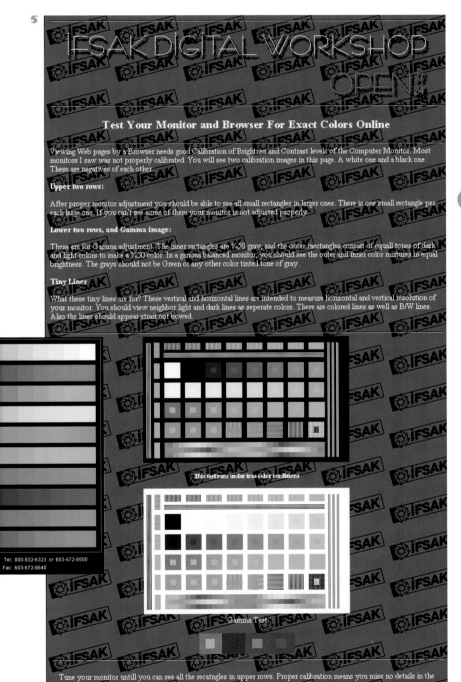

5

IFSAK DIGITAL WORKSHOP
OPEN!

Test Your Monitor and Browser For Exact Colors Online

Viewing Web pages by a Browser needs good Calibration of Brightnes and Contrast levels of the Computer Monitor. Most monitors I saw was not properly calibrated. You will see two calibration images in this page. A white one and a black one. These are negatives of each other.

Upper two rows:

After proper monitor adjustment you should be able to see all small rectangles in larger ones. There is one small rectangle per each large one. If you can't see some of them your monitor is not adjusted properly.

Lower two rows, and Gamma image:

These are for Gamma adjustment. The inner rectangles are %50 gray, and the outer raectangles consist of equall tones of dark and light colors to make a %50 color. In a gamma balanced monitor, you should see the outer and inner color mixtures in equal brightness. The grays should not be Green or any other color tinted tone of gray.

Tiny Lines

What these tiny lines are for? These vertical and horizontal lines are intended to measure horizontal and vertical resolution of your monitor. You should view neighbor light and dark lines as seperate colors. There are colored lines as well as B/W lines. Also the lines should appear strait not bowed.

This test runs under true color conditions

Gamma Test

Tune your monitor untill you can see all the recatngles in upper rows. Proper calibration means you miss no details in the dark and bright edges when viewing web graphics...

Email: info@displaymate.com
Web: www.displaymate.com

DisplayMate Technologies Corp.
Color Scales Test Pattern
©1999 by DisplayMate® Technologies Corp.

Tel: 800-932-6323 or 603-672-8500
Fax: 603-672-8640

COLOUR SCHEMING

Would you drive a purple car? While wearing a lime-green shirt? Would you let someone else tell you what constitutes a good combination of colours? Or let your computer decide it for you? There are complex influences at work in the matter of colour choice. Some of these factors seem to be physiological, but most must be acquired through exposure to a particular outside world. The average citizen may have sensitivities allied to the colour of the national flag. The average Inuit has allegedly more than two dozen words to describe the different colours of snow. The average Web-page designer has 216 colours to describe the appearance of everything in the known universe.

Leaving the difficult matter of taste aside for a moment, there is the additional constraint of the established conventions of link colours. Clickable links have been blue (0000FF) since year zero in the history of the Internet, visited links purple (990099), and active links red (FF0000). These colour settings are easily changeable, but at the risk of confusing the viewer.

In the interests of humanity, 140 colours of the Web palette have been blessed with names – and can be defined in more recent browsers by using those names rather than hexadecimal numbers. Earlier browsers will only respond to a select ten from this named list. None of the above gives any clue as to a strategy for choosing colours, though the Web authoring-software packages sometimes kindly group colours by related hue values. Here we are in a purple car, wearing a lime-green shirt and wondering what looks nice. Enough prevarication. Nothing is to be lost by trial and error – the Web page, unlike the domestic interior, has an infinite capacity for absorbing ill-judged decisions. Take a published site that has a good colour sense and analyse the HTML colours. Go a step further and borrow that colour scheme; then change the colour values one by one.

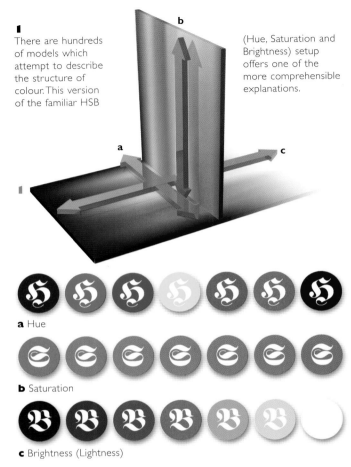

There are hundreds of models which attempt to describe the structure of colour. This version of the familiar HSB (Hue, Saturation and Brightness) setup offers one of the more comprehensible explanations.

a Hue

b Saturation

c Brightness (Lightness)

Soon it will be obvious which are the pivotal colours at the heart of the scheme. Also, that it is colour contrast, rather than the nature of the colours themselves, that's at the root of successful colour selection. Prove it by making a screen grab of a good site and inverting the colours in an image-editing program. Chances are, though it may appear strange, it still hangs together.

Try returning to the familiar artist's colour wheel for a from-the-ground-up view of how colour choice works; or visit Hot Door (at **www.hotdoor.com**) for a trial of their Harmony software (*opposite*). Above all, remember that the viewer's eyeballs are temporarily in your care.

Automating the decision

The hard business of colour choice can be mechanized with the aid of a replacement colour picker attached to the image-editing or Web authoring-software. HotDoor Harmony offers such a regime in the form of a replacement Photoshop colour picker (2), with combinations of two to six colours. The underlying logic is the artist's colour wheel – with an added shot of roulette.

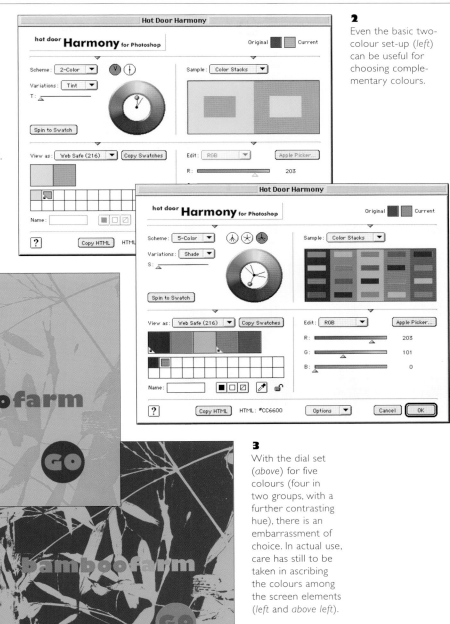

2
Even the basic two-colour set-up (*left*) can be useful for choosing comple-mentary colours.

3
With the dial set (*above*) for five colours (four in two groups, with a further contrasting hue), there is an embarrassment of choice. In actual use, care has still to be taken in ascribing the colours among the screen elements (*left* and *above left*).

CHINESE WHISPERS

After the close control of paper publishing, designing by Chinese Whispers over the Web is daunting. The whisper starts in Adobe Photoshop, perhaps, passing through exotic plug-ins before it reaches the Web page. When served back to the reader, it transits through a browser of indeterminate age and pedigree on anything from a high-end graphics workstation to a palm-sized portable. It is not so much a matter of retaining control, as knowing how not to lose it completely.

The choice is to opt for either 'safe colour' or full colour. Constrained to a 'safe' palette of just 216 colours chosen by arithmetic rather than aesthetics, graphics should pass fairly faithfully to the eye of the beholder. Images with continuous tones can only truly be safe if you are sure that the beholder will have more than 256 colours (8-bit colour depth); such full colour still requires careful preparation to ensure acceptably brief download times.

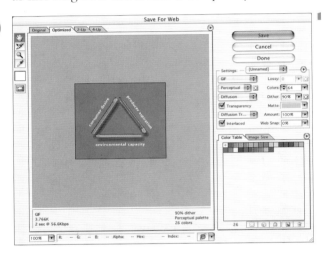

1

Your starting point may be the same as for printed work, but to get the best out of your pictures you'll need some added tools and skills. Photoshop's Save For Web command (in the File menu) offers fine control over colour and the format of GIF files – including the use of transparency – and provides inter-lacing. This slices the image, TV style, into two sets of horizontal lines. The arrival of the first set can reassure the viewer that the download is in progress, the second fills in the missing areas to sharpen up the image.

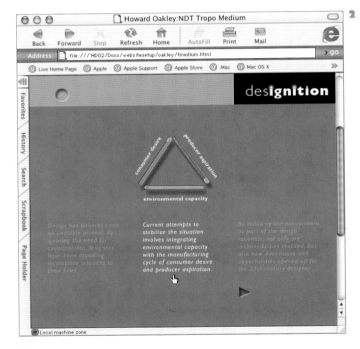

2

You have no control over the browser or platform on which a user will render your pages. Transparency could work well, as shown here in a recent version of Internet Explorer, but older browsers may not cope with it. You need to decide how well you support legacy systems, and then design and test accordingly.

3

HTML has scant support for colour. It simply links the contents of a page together, leaving the recipient to render embedded graphics. Mark-up commands can colour text, backgrounds and borders, but even there you should take care to keep to cross-platform standards.

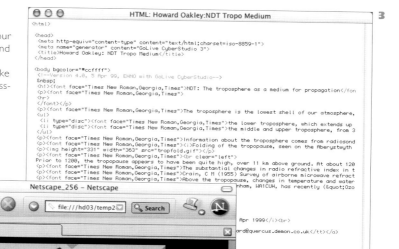

4

Previewed using just 256 colours, this page appears quite readable in Netscape Navigator on a Mac.

5

Moving up to 'millions of colours', the colours in the graphic have desaturated but remain quite acceptable. However, the purple used to identify links has become too bright, making the text unreadable – some-thing not seen in the authoring software. Check everything offline before going live, so problems can be traced through the sequence of whispers and corrected.

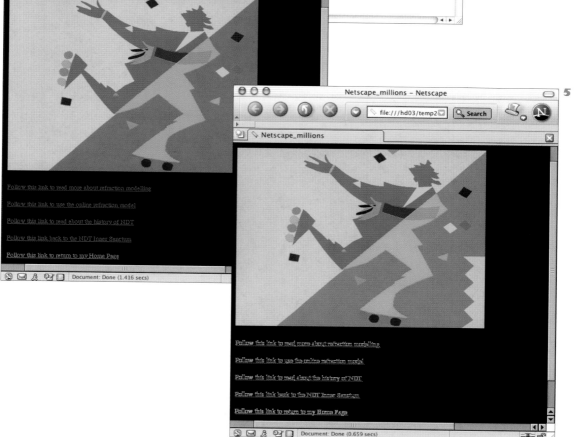

SAFETY FIRST

Careful planning and a degree of experimentation are necessary for the execution of a 'safe' colour regime. In the right hands, graphic-design work constrained to the 216 colours of the safe palette can look perfectly natural and remain every bit as good as unconstrained work.

Do not be afraid to employ dithering, either to enrich solid areas of colour with the illusion of a third dimension or to extend the perceived range of colours beyond the 216. Whilst dithering can detract from photographic images (particularly if performed on the viewer's computer), its skilful use in digital drawings can be very effective.

Dithering can also help you through strict colour rules that clients may impose on logos and their ilk. At the outset, you should establish clear ground rules as to how you will achieve compliance, and then take great care to match colours.

1 | 2 | 3 | 4 | 5
The process of reducing the colour palette of an image – as in the 216 'Web-safe' palette – produces an effect of flat, hard-edged colour bands (1). To compensate for the reduced palette you can use the technique of 'dithering', in which the image pixels are redistributed in a predetermined pattern to create the illusion of a smooth transition from one colour to another. Dithered patterns can be styled 'diffusion', a random pattern that can be applied in variable amounts (2, with 50% dithering and 3, with 100%), 'pattern' – a regular matrix of pixels (4) or 'noise' – randomly placed pixels that decrease image definition (5).

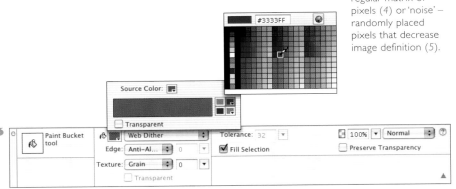

6
Make sure that all the graphics and Web design applications that you use can display the Web-safe colour palette. Although most are supplied with this as standard, you may need to make your own if using utilities such as, for example, GraphicConverter Photoshop and Fireworks both include 216-colour dithering features amongst their optimization tools (see *opposite*), while Fireworks steps ahead with a dedicated feature for creating custom dithered fills: the Web Dither option in the Fill Menu as shown here.

8

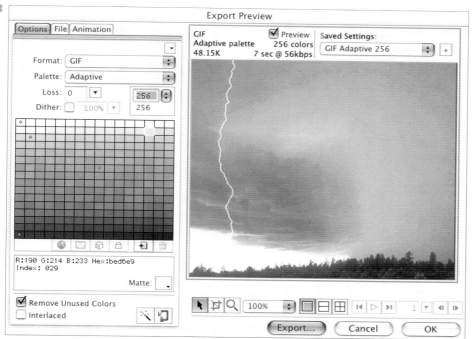

8
Fireworks' Export Preview is a powerful tool for previewing the effects of palette changes and dithering on images. This photograph has been rendered using an adaptive palette of 256 colours. Because its continuous tones cover a limited range of colours, it still looks very smooth and true to the original. Although not Web-safe, some adaptive palettes stand less chance of being significantly misrendered on client systems.

9

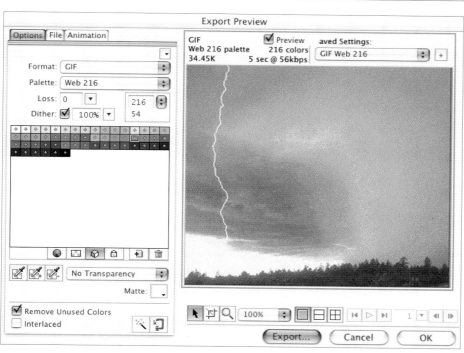

9
Dithered into safe colours, the sky breaks up into a mess of patches, some with obvious diagonal banding. In most cases, this type of image is best kept in deeper colour (e.g. 32-bit JPEG), risking poor rendering only if the viewer's system can offer a mere 256 colours.

LOSS PREVENTION

Whether you're working with the continuous tones of photographic images (or digital painting) or drawings from desktop design software, Photoshop is a reliable and capable starting point for colour work. Armed with the right plug-ins and techniques, its vast capabilities can almost always help you to find a way through problems.

When working with pictures, you should store them using a non-lossy format, such as Photoshop native files, and only apply lossy compression methods such as JPEG as the final step before placing the pictures in Web pages. Repeatedly saving a file with JPEG compression – which discards information at each 'save' – results in progressively deteriorating image quality.

Safe colour images should be converted to indexed colour (rather than RGB colour) at an early stage, so that they remain within the safe palette. Moreover, because GIF compression doesn't discard any data, you can safely keep working files using that format.

Because mainstream Web graphics can't accommodate Postscript's fonts, curves and colour handling, Photoshop's built-in Postscript engine is also an invaluable tool for rendering EPS files created using Postscript design tools such as Adobe Illustrator and Macromedia Freehand.

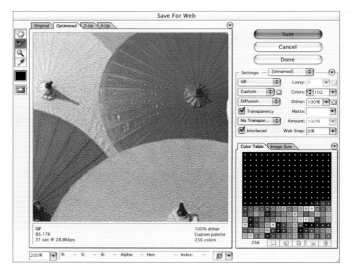

1
To create and save a safe colour GIF in Photoshop, start with an RGB colour picture.

2
Next use Photoshop's Save For Web command in the File menu to display the Export dialogue. The window shows a preview of your optimized image, while the Settings box on the right provides the control you need. Choose one of the settings in the top drop-down menu, then use the various controls to get the result you want.

3

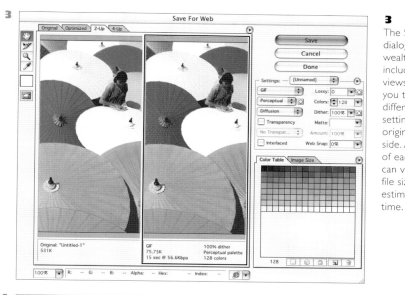

3
The Save For Web dialogue offers a wealth of options, include 2- and 4-up views, which enable you to compare different export settings and the original image side by side. At the bottom of each preview, you can view the output file size and an estimated download time.

4

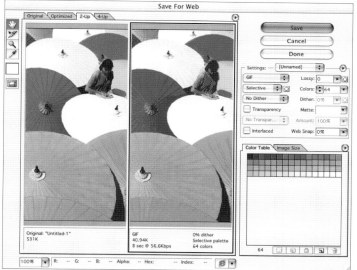

5

6

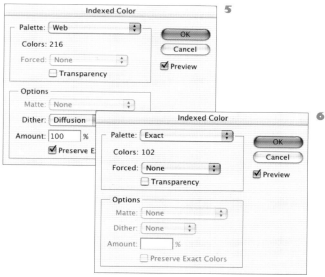

4
You can dramatically reduce the file size of an image – and therefore speed up the download time – by experimenting with different optimization settings. The amount of colour in the image is the key factor, while dithering itself may substantially increase the file size.

5 | 6
One drawback to the Save For Web workspace is you cannot directly edit the image here. If you want to work on an image and view the result with a particular set of colours at the same time, set it to Indexed colour mode – you'll find this in Photoshop's Image>Mode menu.

LABOUR SAVING

The legacy of nearly two decades of on-screen page make-up activity is a vast amount of that most precious commodity – content. The traditions of print mean there is an equally large amount of redundancy locked up in this material. From the Web perspective, there are billions of words with an excess of typographic styling and similar numbers of images of unnecessarily high resolution. A combination of three routes is the key to unlocking the potential of these pages. At a simple level, 'old' pages can be turned into EPS files and re-manufactured into Web-ready GIFs. This crude approach mostly results in disaster, with reduced definition

mangling the words, though images can survive this treatment reasonably intact. Further up the scale of effort, text content can be remade into HTML and the accompanying images brought out of CMYK into RGB at lower resolution. The most sophisticated solution is now provided by later versions of the original page make-up applications. This software offers an interface which comfortably mimics the print-based techniques, while producing Web-ready output rather than files for film. Similar changes have taken place among the vector-based drawing applications. They now include animation and powerful image optimization capabilities.

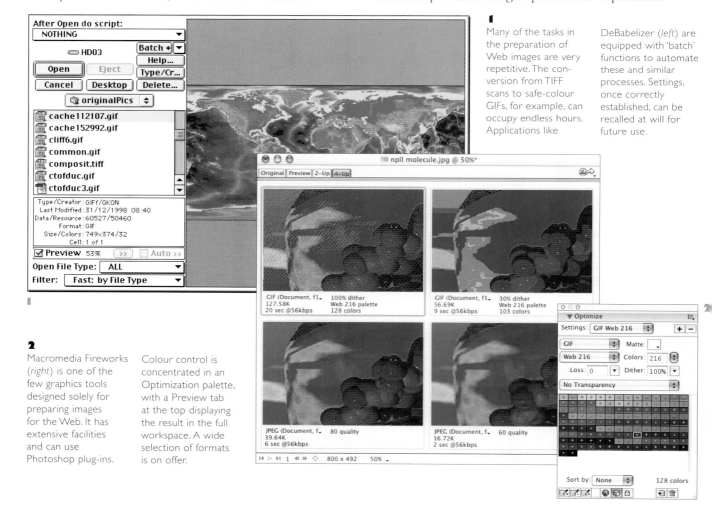

1
Many of the tasks in the preparation of Web images are very repetitive. The conversion from TIFF scans to safe-colour GIFs, for example, can occupy endless hours. Applications like

DeBabelizer (*left*) are equipped with 'batch' functions to automate these and similar processes. Settings, once correctly established, can be recalled at will for future use.

2
Macromedia Fireworks (*right*) is one of the few graphics tools designed solely for preparing images for the Web. It has extensive facilities and can use Photoshop plug-ins.

Colour control is concentrated in an Optimization palette, with a Preview tab at the top displaying the result in the full workspace. A wide selection of formats is on offer.

3 | 4

Early versions of Freehand, and its rival, Illustrator, were used for vector-based drawing. These and other applications have now moved into the territory of the painting programs. Type effects in Freehand (*left*) can now be combined with bitmap manipulation. Note the colour palette (*far left*) with safe colours loaded from a built-in library. The result can be previewed (*above*) via the application in a browser of your choice.

5 | 6

ImageReady is now included in the Photoshop package. Pages developed in the main application can be optimized for screen display in the companion software (*left*). The page is sliced into sections (*below left*), so that various compression settings can be tried. The main image is being tested at progressively coarser JPEG settings. The remaining graphic has been saved as a small GIF file, while the background areas make even smaller files, saved as single-colour 'no image' slices.

7 | 8

The banding in the ImageReady colour picker (*above*) demonstrates the limitations of the Web-safe palette when compared with the full-colour version.

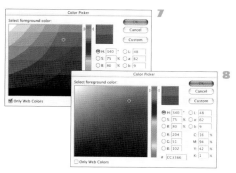

PAINTING BY NUMBERS

Although HTML is hardly colour-centred, it does support limited use of colour in text, backgrounds and borders. Used judiciously, such colour can be both aesthetically pleasing and safe across browsers and platforms. The same rule applies as for GIF pictures: confine colours to those in the palette of 216. However, in their effort to boast yet more features, major Web-authoring software packages offer a profusion of colour palettes, as if to drag you away from safe colour.

1
Dreamweaver offers standard HTML colour schemes as style sheets. Whilst these are guaranteed Web-safe, there are many more combinations – which can be equally effective and may appear less hackneyed. Each of the colours within these schemes is safe, not just the combinations that are offered.

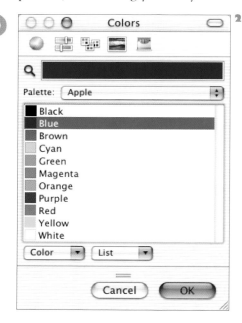

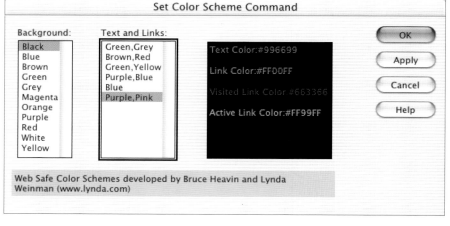

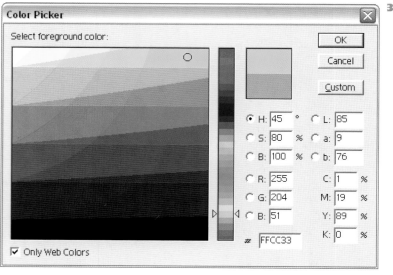

2
If you decide to use an authoring software package that doesn't offer such built-in facilities, or prefer to hand-roll your own raw HTML, there are still tools to aid the safe use of colour. SafePicker shows you numeric colour values and helps you to paste them into HTML documents.

3
You might find it easier to evolve a colour scheme in your graphics application. You can constrain Photoshop's colour picker to display Web-safe colours only, using the checkbox at the bottom left. The box at the bottom right, marked #, gives the HTML code for your selected colour.

4 | 5 | 6

Don't be tempted to use browser-specific named colours. Very few of them migrate successfully. Instead, keep to colours that are defined numerically, which cannot be misinterpreted by the HTML rendering engine in a browser. For instance, #FFFFFF is pure white and #000000 is black. In the example, right, the nearest colour to 'Cornflower blue' (4) is '#6699FF' (5). When offered by the package, HTML parsing and checking (6) should help spot any errors in your code – though you will probably still need to check that your colours are Web-safe.

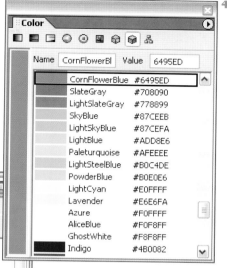

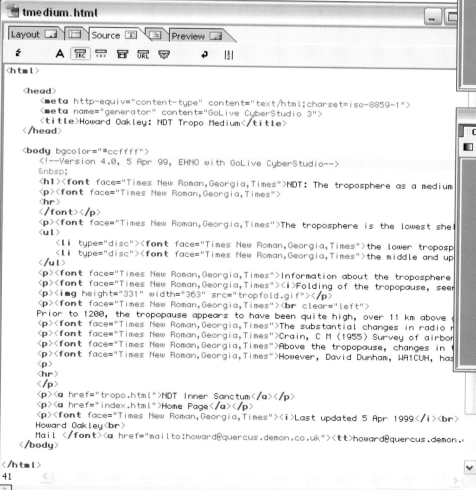

```html
<html>

    <head>
        <meta http-equiv="content-type" content="text/html;charset=iso-8859-1">
        <meta name="generator" content="GoLive CyberStudio 3">
        <title>Howard Oakley: NDT Tropo Medium</title>
    </head>

    <body bgcolor="#ccffff">
        <!--Version 4.0, 5 Apr 99, EHNO with GoLive CyberStudio-->
         
        <h1><font face="Times New Roman,Georgia,Times">NDT: The troposphere as a medium
        <p><font face="Times New Roman,Georgia,Times">
        <hr>
        </font></p>
        <p><font face="Times New Roman,Georgia,Times">The troposphere is the lowest she
        <ul>
            <li type="disc"><font face="Times New Roman,Georgia,Times">the lower troposp
            <li type="disc"><font face="Times New Roman,Georgia,Times">the middle and up
        </ul>
        <p><font face="Times New Roman,Georgia,Times">Information about the troposphere
        <p><font face="Times New Roman,Georgia,Times"><i>Folding of the tropopause, seer
        <p><img height="331" width="363" src="tropfold.gif"></p>
        <p><font face="Times New Roman,Georgia,Times"><br clear="left">
        Prior to 1200, the tropopause appears to have been quite high, over 11 km above
        <p><font face="Times New Roman,Georgia,Times">The substantial changes in radio
        <p><font face="Times New Roman,Georgia,Times">Crain, C M (1955) Survey of airbor
        <p><font face="Times New Roman,Georgia,Times">Above the tropopause, changes in t
        <p><font face="Times New Roman,Georgia,Times">However, David Dunham, WA1CUH, has
        <p>
        <hr>
        </p>
        <p><a href="tropo.html">NDT Inner Sanctum</a></p>
        <p><a href="index.html">Home Page</a></p>
        <p><font face="Times New Roman,Georgia,Times"><i>Last updated 5 Apr 1999</i><br>
        Howard Oakley<br>
        Mail </font><a href="mailto:howard@quercus.demon.co.uk"><tt>howard@quercus.demon.
    </body>

</html>
```

PHOTO QUALITY

The overwhelming majority of Web graphics are in JPEG or GIF format, despite the aspirations of the newer PNG specification and other contenders. As no single format yet meets the 'one size fits all' requirement to supplant JPEG and GIF, this is likely to change slowly.

JPEG, often condensed into the MS-DOS extension .jpg, was designed to store continuous tone colour images, such as photographs and painted artwork, in space-efficient form. Because, to save space, its compression method simplifies the image content, it should serve as the final output format, and not be used for intermediate storage when working on images. The severity of compression is variable, with smaller file sizes resulting in poorer-quality images: you should therefore, if your software permits, preview the effect of different degrees of compression before making a final commitment.

JPEG will effectively anti-alias sharp edges in the image and is thus rarely suitable for line art or digital drawings. In these cases, GIF is normally preferred, as it retains sharp edges and will not of itself cause anti-aliasing. Indeed, softening JPEG images with a gentle blurring filter can help them compress better.

JPEG retains full colour information at 24-bit depth ('millions of colours') and has no facility for reducing the number of colours. However, it can contain information about image resolution, so you should ensure that the final output resolution is set to 72 dots per inch (dpi).

Progressive JPEG is a variant that works similarly to interlaced GIF in that the image is previewed during download, in blurry form; as it is not supported by Netscape browsers earlier than version 2.0 or Internet Explorer prior to 3.0, its use could result in a missing image on some systems.

1 | 2

You can save Photoshop images in the ordinary way as JPEGs – just select JPEG in the Form dropdown in the Save dialogue. But the JPEG Options dialog this provides (*above*) doesn't offer the visual feedback and level of control you get with the Save From Web command (*right*). This latter is very similar to the one in Fireworks: both offer a quality slider, which reduces file size in tandem with quality.

42

3 | 4 | 5 | 6

JPEG is a file format that uses a 'lossy' compression method, meaning that some image data – and thus quality – may be lost during compression. The advantage of the JPEG format is that it can be used to display images in millions of colours rather than in the limited palette of GIF (which uses 'lossless' compression techniques) and other formats. The degree of compression can be defined by you, but the more you apply, the poorer the quality of displayed image. The examples show an image with varying amounts of compression, along with the original, uncompressed image (3). The quality of JPEG images is measured as a percentage of maximum or on a scale of 0–12, the latter divided into quality categories of low (0–4), medium (5–7), high (8–9) and maximum (10–12). At settings of high or maximum, image degradation is virtually unnoticeable, but at medium becomes more apparent (4, with a setting of 6). At low settings quality becomes very noticeable (5, set at 3), and at the lowest, 0, images become virtually unusable (6).

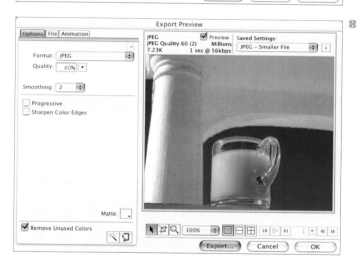

7

Good-quality JPEG images can still be quite compact – here, downloadable over a 'standard' slow dial-up connection in 20 seconds. The image is sharp, with excellent colour reproduction when viewed on a suitable system (one with more than 256 colours available).

8

Halving the file size, to download in only 9 seconds, has a significant effect on the sharpness; but little on the colour. Given the transient nature of the Web, you need to ask yourself how long a viewer will study the image and what quality is needed, so you can choose the right compromise between download speed and quality. But by opting for JPEG, you run the risk of viewers with only 256 colours being disappointed by the rendering of the picture.

43

CONCENTRATED COLOUR

GIF files use indexed colour constrained to no more than 8 bits in depth (256 colours or less), making them ideal for safe colour use. They employ a non-lossy compression method that is most effective when dealing with long runs of the same colour horizontally along a row; vertical patterns, dithering and anti-aliasing in the image will therefore result in larger file sizes.

Optional features that can be used in GIFs include interlacing and transparency, with or without an alpha channel. Interlacing is popular for those with slower Internet connections, as it shows a blurry preview image early during download, progressively gaining resolution. Transparency is effective for displaying non-rectangular images, and can either key to the background colour (in which case you must avoid using that colour in the heart of the image) or use an alpha channel.

Early concerns over parts of the GIF format that are covered by patents fuelled the development of the PNG standard for colour images 8, 24 or 32 bits deep. Although it is not supported by many browsers and does not work as well as JPEG on photographic images, it attempts to correct for the screen gamma.

1
Undithered GIF images can appear posterized, which, although occasionally attractive, are invariably not, since perspective and clarity may be weakened, requiring you to soften edges between areas of solid colour.

2

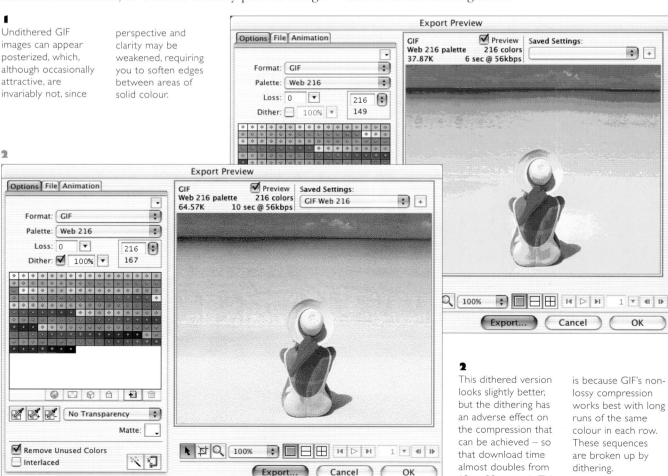

2
This dithered version looks slightly better, but the dithering has an adverse effect on the compression that can be achieved – so that download time almost doubles from 12 to 22 seconds. This is because GIF's non-lossy compression works best with long runs of the same colour in each row. These sequences are broken up by dithering.

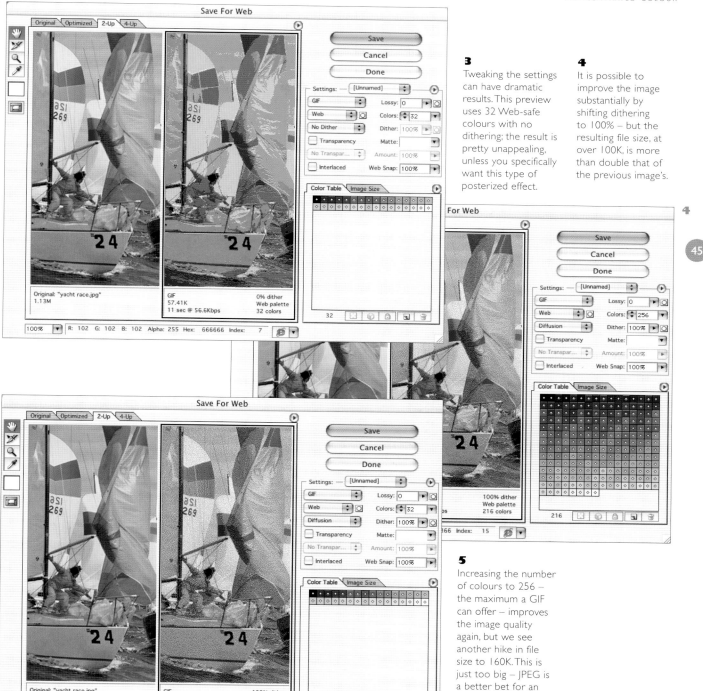

3
Tweaking the settings can have dramatic results. This preview uses 32 Web-safe colours with no dithering; the result is pretty unappealing, unless you specifically want this type of posterized effect.

4
It is possible to improve the image substantially by shifting dithering to 100% – but the resulting file size, at over 100K, is more than double that of the previous image's.

5
Increasing the number of colours to 256 – the maximum a GIF can offer – improves the image quality again, but we see another hike in file size to 160K. This is just too big – JPEG is a better bet for an image like this.

TESTING THE MARGINS

Given the contrasting approaches adopted by JPEG and GIF, you will normally not have difficulty deciding which is more appropriate. However, making the choice is not always easy, and cannot always be based on the nature of the picture and the expected download time. When preparing a number of similar pictures, experiment with one or two to see how well they work when compressed and then rendered, using the two methods. With JPEG in particular, try different levels of compression, and check the results at different colour depths and on different systems.

If there is any risk that a browser will not be able to render a picture, give a clue as to what it is missing, using the ALT mark-up in HTML (essential if the image functions as key information, an active button – or, most of all, an image map, providing a text-only alternative). Badly rendered colour is preferable to broken picture links which could make your pages unusable.

1 This photograph is quite adequately rendered in just 256 colours, using an adaptive palette that is far from Web-safe. You might risk that palette on an Intranet where you know the browsers and hardware platforms, but it could suffer terribly in the hands of an old Windows 3 system.

2

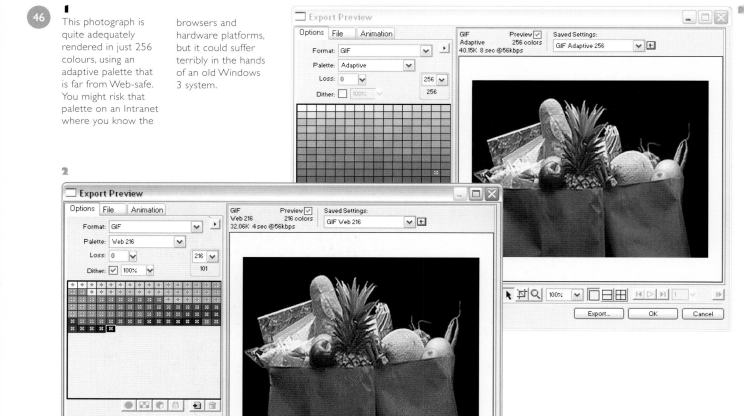

2 Dithered into the safe palette, the image becomes visibly too grainy, and will consequently compress relatively poorly. Instead of taking 12 seconds to download to the hypothetical standard client, it would take 8 seconds.

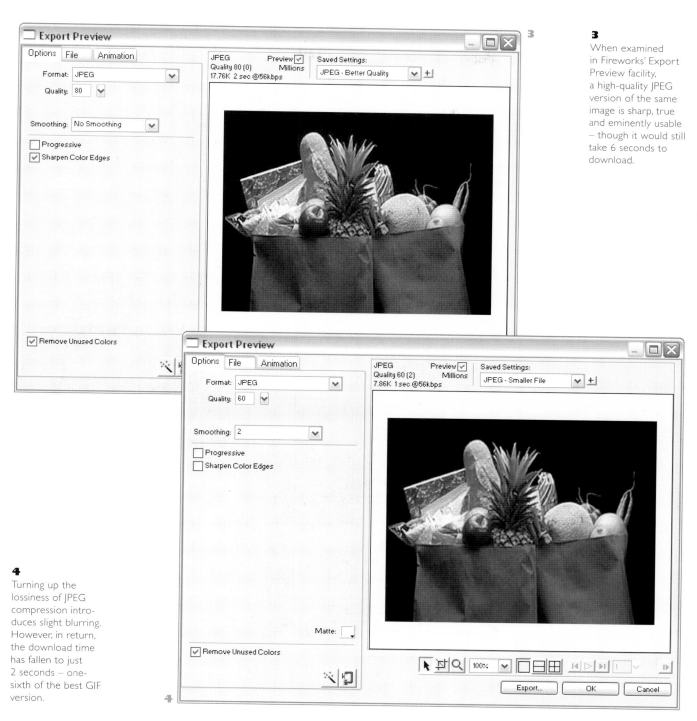

3
When examined in Fireworks' Export Preview facility, a high-quality JPEG version of the same image is sharp, true and eminently usable – though it would still take 6 seconds to download.

4
Turning up the lossiness of JPEG compression introduces slight blurring. However, in return, the download time has fallen to just 2 seconds – one-sixth of the best GIF version.

TONAL VARIATIONS

In contrast to printed media, continuous-tone mono-chrome images on the Web pose more problems than they solve. In the 216 safe colours, there are but four greys between black and white; even skilfully dithered, most images will look crude. Although much easier with a palette of 256 greys, all except six would be unsafe and could get rendered incorrectly on many monitors. Thus, high-quality monochrome work demands the full-colour approach – so the attraction of potentially smaller file sizes is illusory.

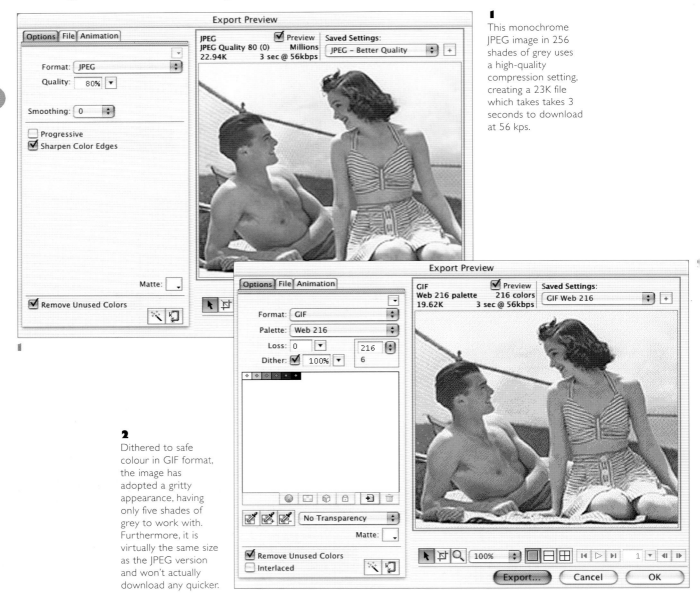

1
This monochrome JPEG image in 256 shades of grey uses a high-quality compression setting, creating a 23K file which takes takes 3 seconds to download at 56 kps.

2
Dithered to safe colour in GIF format, the image has adopted a gritty appearance, having only five shades of grey to work with. Furthermore, it is virtually the same size as the JPEG version and won't actually download any quicker.

48

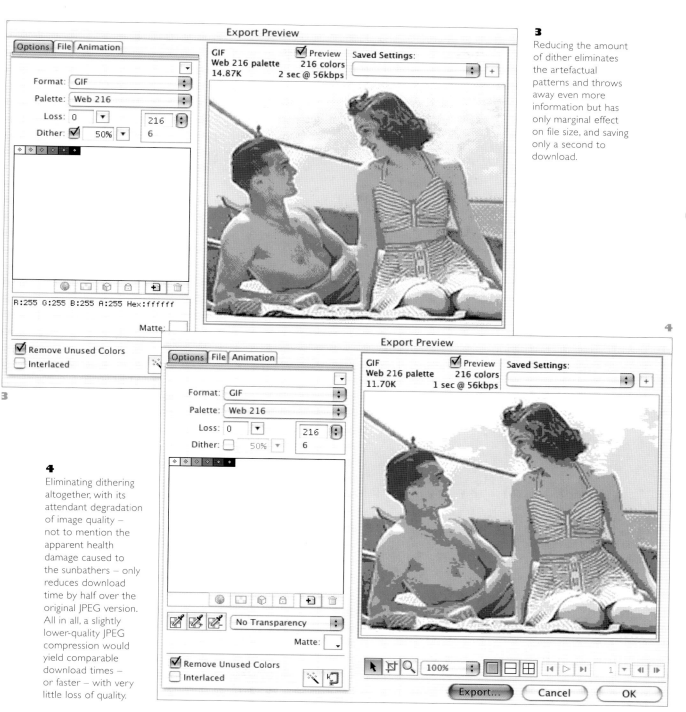

3

Reducing the amount of dither eliminates the artefactual patterns and throws away even more information but has only marginal effect on file size, and saving only a second to download.

4

Eliminating dithering altogether, with its attendant degradation of image quality – not to mention the apparent health damage caused to the sunbathers – only reduces download time by half over the original JPEG version. All in all, a slightly lower-quality JPEG compression would yield comparable download times – or faster – with very little loss of quality.

THROUGH A GLASS DARKLY

In the controlled and ordered printed medium, you wouldn't commit to print before satisfying yourself that proofs were up to the required standard and faithful in colour reproduction. Electronic proofing for the Web requires that you view your finished pages on Windows and Mac OS (if not Unix/Linux) machines, using at least the two most popular browsers, Netscape and Microsoft Internet Explorer, in a range of different versions.

An immediately obvious difference will be between gamma values: whilst Windows systems usually operate at 2.2, Mac OS and most Unix boxes have a gamma less than 2.0 (as low as 1.7 on Silicon Graphics computers). Images that appeared balanced on a Mac are therefore going to appear darker, when viewed under Windows. Alternatively, if you adjusted them to look right under Windows, then they will appear too light on Macs. There is no easy solution, although the PNG graphics format attempts to perform gamma correction. Most designers end up working to a gamma of around 2.0 to 2.2, but this should be modified to take your most important users into account.

When performing electronic proofing, you need to check your pages at high and low colour depths, typically 24-bit ('millions of colours') and 8-bit (256 colours). When restricted to 256 colours (the main reason for keeping to the Web-safe palette of 216), forced dithering can be much poorer than that achieved during design.

50

Viewed in Internet Explorer on a Mac, using the standard Mac gamma of 1.8, the detail in this rather dark picture looks fine.

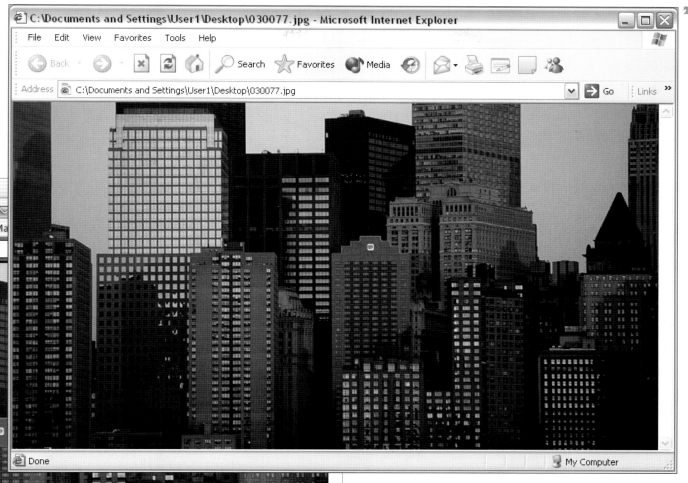

2

This is how a Windows user, with a gamma of 2.2, would see the same picture – with detail beginning to disappear in the darker parts of the image. The picture should be adjusted so that it looks right at a gamma of around 2.0, the best compromise for a mixed audience.

PROOF POSITIVE

Printed versions of Web pages are potentially important records of your work, perhaps the only way of committing the ephemeral to more permanent form. However, you need to reverse the process commonly used to import images into Web pages: to achieve faithful reproduction, you must transpose RGB images to CMYK. Although not easy on any system, ColorSync on the Mac OS is a clear advantage here, provided that you have built appropriate colour profiles for your different output devices (your monitor and printer, at least).

Nor are Web browsers ideal applications from which to print. They struggle to hold sensible page sizes, and have suffered notorious bugs in the past. Web-authoring packages are not a good solution either, due to the limitations in their HTML rendering. Probably the best option currently available is to convert the relevant pages, or the complete Web site, into an Adobe Acrobat document and print that.

1 | 2 | 3
Unambitious page design (*1*) has its virtues when the time comes to print. The Disney page appears faultlessly on a mid-range colour inkjet printer (*2*), and the inherent colour contrast of the original helps it to survive even in black-and-white (*3*).

4 | 5 | 6
Under the same conditions, the Jewel page (4) breaks into unappealing lumps (5, 6). As usual in the music business, if you want a souvenir, you'll have to buy the T-shirt.

PICTURE THIS

Now that the 2.7-million-pixel digital camera is no longer a novelty, there are more pixels washing around than can be decently used in a currently average Web image. The pictures on this page exaggerate the point, but we are still some way off being able to transmit large (and magnifiable) images across the Web.

1 | 2
The landscape (*left, with detail, above*) is a composite: the left-hand side comes from a camera costing the same as a decent used family car – the right from one approximating the value of a reasonable meal for four people. The lower half of the image has been sharpened, and enhanced with Auto Levels. The close-up shows obvious differences, but the browser window (reproduced at actual size from a 1024 x 768 pixel screen) renders the whole scene virtually as one.

3

3 | 4

Some after-treatment of the photographic image pays off. The original (3) was shot through a window clad with an amber anti-sun filter. Before producing JPEGs for screen use (4), a simple application of the Auto Curves filter cleaned up most of the colour cast and lack of contrast. The JPEGs retain the skin tones reasonably well; only the GIF begins to show banding, though this is less offensive than the murky tones of the untreated half.

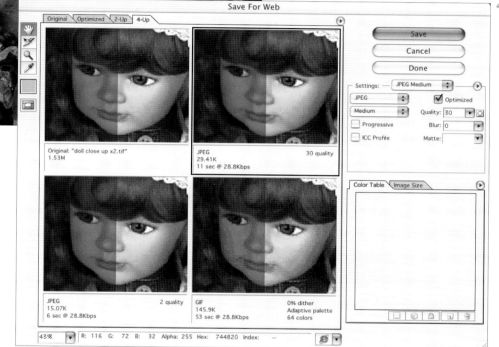

4

7

5

5 | 6 | 7

A perfectly reasonable photograph (5) can be submitted to the traditional Photoshop manipulations (6). The jury is out on whether these effects represent an improvement, but a fragment of the Photoshop History palette (7) gives an idea of the necessary manœuvres.

6

SWIMMING AGAINST THE TIDE

The business of threading coloured images through the narrow eye of the file-size needle gets tedious at times. The pressure is always on to retain as much as possible of the quality of the original item. Or maybe not. There are opportunities to take advantage of the limitations of dither, GIF and JPEG.

Whether you are using scanned images or digital photographs, like these, the apparently perverse first step is to ensure that the maximum amount of useful colour information is retained. First, filters like Intellihance can be used to extract the maximum from the image; then creative degradation can begin.

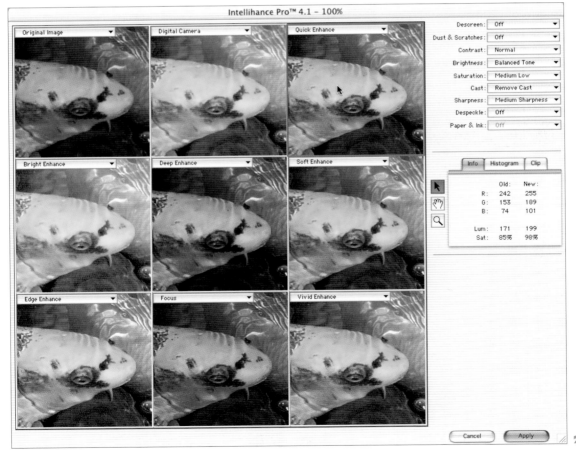

1 | 2
The original digital image (*above*) is treated in Intellihance to a number of variations (*left*). There are a further 14 available, each of which can be customized to suit a particular task.

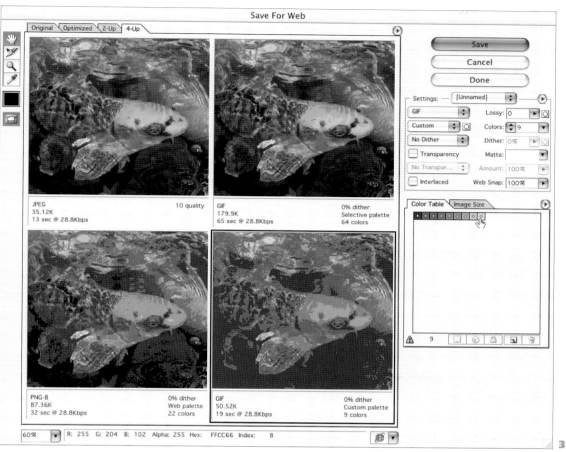

3 | 4 | 5 | 6

Photoshop's 'Save for Web' command (*3*) offers an array of permutations before saving the image as a Web-ready document. The panel shows variations on the three available formats – the highlighted file demonstrates that the old adage about GIFs being no good for tonal images is only partly true. Further below the surface (*4*), it is clear that dithering should not be dismissed out of hand. Application of Photoshop's Plastic Wrap filter (*5*) and an 8-colour GIF palette leads to interesting effects. The same filter was used in conjunction with hue shifting (*6*) to finally lose touch with the original image.

59

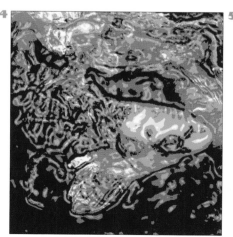

SCANNING FOR SCRAPS

Humble office scanners, so cheap that they may yet be given away with a box of cornflakes, nevertheless have great value in the relatively low-resolution environment of the Web. Flat subjects are obviously the norm, but even a rudimentary scanner has a surprisingly large depth of focus when faced with three-dimensional objects. Looking farther afield, the Web itself is a rich source of visual material – a lot for free, and much more if you're willing to use your charge card.

Even the screen itself can yield useful material for recycling. With the aid of a screen-capture utility and a good deal of dogged persistence, there are surprising effects to be realized.

1
Try making a temporary paper tent over small objects like this corkscrew. With such metallic subjects, the moving scanner lamp will often oblige with curious reflections completely unlike the ones that are produced by conventional photography.

2 | 3 | 4 | 5 | 6
The default scanner setting (2) usually produces a weak result (4). Homing in on the required image (3) achieves better saturation (5). The same image on a digital camera (6) needs colour balancing to retain the original chromolithograph's skin tones.

60

7 | 8 | 9 | 10 | 11

The Eclectic Artistry gallery is shown here to represent the thousands of such sites across the Web that offer visual inspiration. Manet and Monet (9) would be proud to be in this popularizing company, and jealous of the automatic landscape production qualities of Bryce 3D (7). The stirring sky (11) is from a commercial photo CD. The two mysterious shapes (*far right*) are among many that are free to download from the USA's National Institute of Standards and Technology site; they are (8) a scanning electron micrograph of the negative

charge at the tip of a roughness-measuring device, and (10) the damage caused by electrons to a fragment of biosensor film.

Edouardo Manet Monet in His Boat Studio

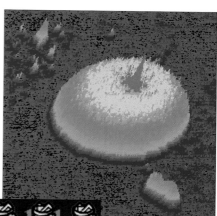

61

12

In the very last resort, try grabbing bits of your own screen. This harmless collage (*left*) was made in Photoshop – entirely from screen captures of these two pages and the under-lying desktop.

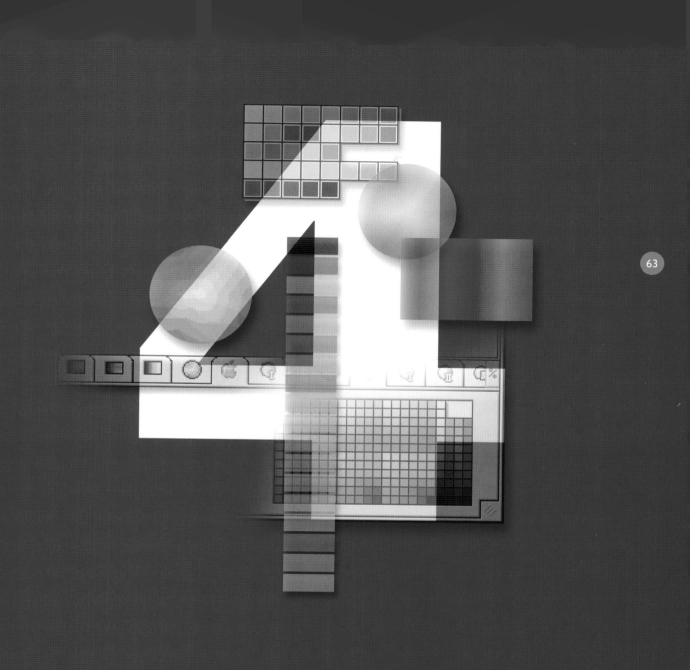

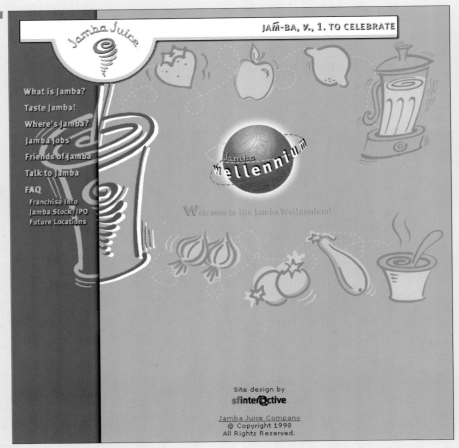

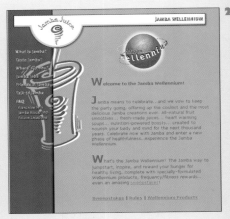

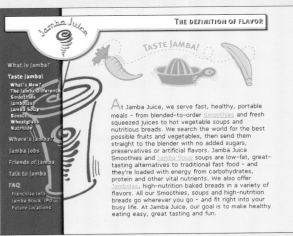

www.jambajuice.com

1 | 2 | 3 | 4

The Jamba Juice splash screen opens up with vibrant tropical-fruit-based colours that are opposite one another on the colour wheel. The 'wellennium planet' bursts open to reveal the 'insides' of the site (1, 2). The strong purple of the opening screen is demoted for use in the opening text. On the following pages a pale-yellow background is selected to keep up the fruit-colour theme – this colour has the advantage of being neutral and of showing up the vivid purple of the text (3, 4). Text links, contrary to the received wisdom, are put into another fruit colour, a bright orange. Raspberry red, tomato red, yellow, orange and green maintain the fruit theme.

5

6

7

www.bridalbabe.com

8

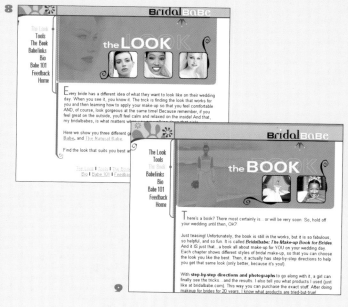

5|6|7|8|9
Bridal Babe uses a narrow range of allied colours, ranging from rose pink and fuchsia to lilac and lavender. These flowery hues help reinforce the atmosphere of ultrafemininity for the nuptial market. The principal drawback in the colour scheme is that these warm colours tend to make the flesh tones look anaemic. Liberal use of a white ground goes some way to balance out this effect. Curlicues and floral motifs evoke an earlier era when 'babe' had a different meaning.

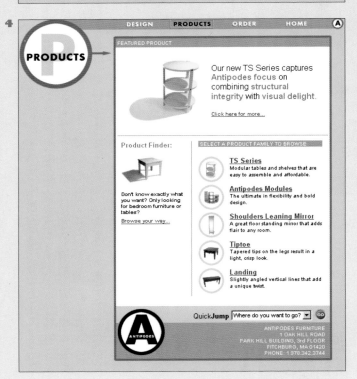

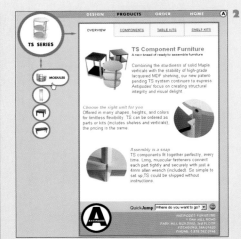

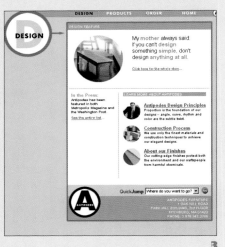

www.antipodesfurniture.com

1 | 2 | 3 | 4
Antipodes Furniture restricts itself to a very limited palette. White, sage green and a narrow khaki band make for a cool and restrained introduction. Product shots are in monotone at microscopic sizes. The recurring circular motif does duty as a magnifying lens to show off the precision of the furniture construction. Solid, restrained design is underlined by the unattributed quotation 'My mother always said "If you can't design something simple, don't design anything at all."' and by the conservative black and dark-blue type. Subheads in the HTML text are coloured to match the restraint of the GIF-based type.

5

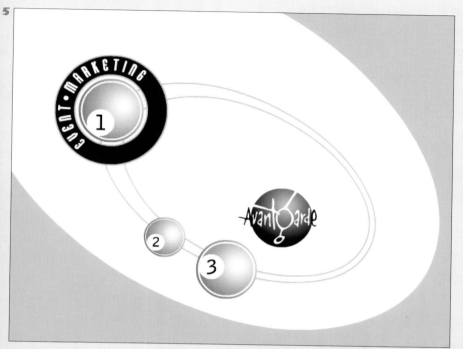

www.avantgarde.com

6

67

7

8

9

5 | 6 | 7 | 8 | 9

Understatement from the world of marketing and PR. What is going on here? This German site demands the Shockwave plug-in, and the little Macromedia banner makes clear the economy of colour in the rest of the site. A shadow effect brings the frame forward; fine vertical lines create the illusion of a third colour, which adds depth to the screen. Further interest is supplied by the engagingly wilful use of a contrasting orange spot colour in the subsequent frames.

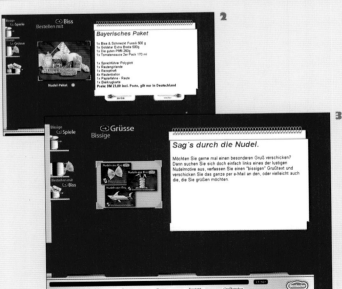

Herzlich
willkommen bei Bernbacher

Navigieren sie mittels Herd durch unser Nudelparadies.
Bernbacher Nudeln – nur echt mit BISS.

Bissige →**Spiele**

Bissige →**Grüsse**

2

1

Bestellen mit →**Biss**

• Wählen Sie ein Kochprogramm ihrer Wahl   13:30•

Bernbacher   Produkte   Rezepte   Presse   Kontakt   Großkunden   Bernbacher

www.bernbacher.de

1 | 2 | 3

What can you do with dried pasta? Lots of interesting shapes but it is all pale yellow. The answer lies in the complementary colour wheel – an ancient pack designer had the right idea. Dark blue is the perfect foil to pale penne – shown here as hero, with the colour contrast between dark blue and yellow making it look inviting. A *tour de force* of silvery-grey JPEGs glamourizes the cooking utensils.

Bayerisches Paket

1x Biss & Schmeckt Fussili 500 g
1x Goldstar Extra Breite 500g
1x Die guten Pfiffi 250g
1x Tomatensauce 2er Pack 170 ml

1x Sprachführer Polyglott
1x Reutengirlande
1x Rezeptheft
4x Rautenballon
1x Papierfahne - Raute
1x Bierkrugkarte
Preis: DM 23,00 incl. Porto, gilt nur in Deutschland

Sag´s durch die Nudel.

Möchten Sie gerne mal einen besonderen Gruß verschicken?
Dann suchen Sie sich doch einfach links eines der lustigen
Nudelmotive aus, verfassen Sie einen "bissigen" Grußtext und
verschicken Sie das ganze per e-Mail an den, oder vielleicht auch
die, Sie grüßen möchten.

4

MODEL RACERS

A new Racing series, just premiered at DiscoverToys. Built for speed, these are collector's items with attitude. All include information about the DiscoverToys Model Racer Society.

price	model		series
		Collect	
$25.50	American classic racer		Custom hot rods
$23.50	Drag race champion		Racing
$25.50	Surf mobile		1950s
$19.95	Racer X		Collector's favorites
$19.95	Rock'n'roll		1950s
$23.50	Roadster		Custom hot rods
$19.95	Blue supertruck		Collector's favorites

5

Remember that sticker album you had as a kid?

Collectibles offer a fascinating journey, bringing together past and future in an ever-evolving community. Collecting brings families and friends together with a shared appreciation of seeing related pieces become whole. Start your collection today…and watch this space for special offers later this summer!

DiscoverToys is an imaginary toy store Web site designed and produced by 415 Productions demonstrating Macromedia products. It requires the latest Flash and Shockwave Players and doesn't actually allow you to buy things like a Mutato-Head (of course, you're encouraged to try!).

69

4|5|6|7

Warm and cosy on the Collectibles toys site; strong yellows and marigolds invite the viewer to linger in a reverie of real or imagined nostalgia. The blue of the text sings out to the prospective purchaser with an irresistible intensity.

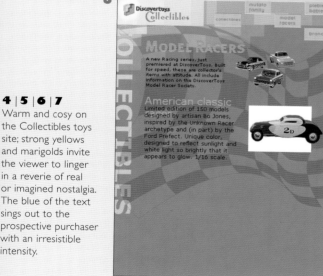

6

MODEL RACERS

A new Racing series, just premiered at DiscoverToys. Built for speed, these are collector's items with attitude. All include information on the DiscoverToys Model Racer Society.

American classic

Limited edition of 150 models designed by artisan Bo Jones, inspired by the Unknown Racer archetype and (in part) by the Ford Prefect. Unique color, designed to reflect sunlight and white light so brightly that it appears to glow. 1/16 scale.

7

MODEL RACERS

A new Racing series, just premiered at DiscoverToys. Built for speed, these are collector's items with attitude. All include information on the DiscoverToys Model Racer Society.

American classic racer

First edition of a new Racing series, just premiered at Disco Toys. Built for speed, this is a collector's item with attitude. Custom paint has a scratch-resistant coating, to protect t car in actual play-race contex Includes information on the Discover Toys Model Racer Society. Alternate Design

www.discovertoys.com

70

Passion in a touch... perfection in a cup... summer in a spoon... One perfect moment.

WHAT'S NEW Häagen-Dazs

Buy an Ice Cream Heart Cake and Get a Free Tube of Frosting

What you write is none of our business! Get the details.

Send a Card from Monte Carlo

Or other dream destinations. Free International Moment e-cards are all new.

New! Ice Cream Flavours to Savour

Allow us to introduce new Créme Caramel Pecan and Mango ice cream.

New! Frozen Yogurt Flavours are Truly Tempting

ry Dulce de Leche and Strawberry frozen yogurt soon, and sigh.

Enter the world of **QUALITY** ice cream and see why we believe Häagen-Dazs is the finest. Sample our ice cream, sorbet, frozen yogurt and other wonderful **PRODUCTS**. Explore the magic of Häagen-Dazs at home with fine **SERVING IDEAS**. Find our **SHOPS & CAFES** around the globe. Look in on our **CLUBS** for offers available only to Häagen-Dazs devotees. Welcome.

GET PERFECT BYTES BY E-MAIL
News, ideas and other wonderful things via e-mail. Subscribe here.

JOIN THE PERFECT REWARDS™ PROGRAM
Special offers, new product news, and more by postal mail. (Available only in the U.S.)

VISIT THE HÄAGEN-DAZS JAPAN SITE

www.haagen-dazs.com

1 | 2 | 3

Häagen-Dazs is rightly feted in the annals of brand promotion for single-mindedness and devotion to core values. The name is a linguistic construct, at once vaguely Scandinavian (for the cool ice-cream values) and mysterious (for an exotic and luxurious feel). A vanilla background and a texture borrowed from the product packaging make a cool foil to the small and seductive ice-cream shots.

VING IDEAS

Dessert Recipes
Drink Recipes
Presentation
Garnishes
Storing and Serving

Dessert Recipes

BAKED ALASKAN SNOWBALLS

BISCOTTI PISTACHIO DESSERT

CAFFE MOCHA SEMIFREDDO

CHERRY SUNDAES IN CHOCOLATE MOUSSE SHELLS

CHOCOLATE 'N FRUIT PHYLLO TARTLETS

CHOCOLATE SHORTCAKE WITH STRAWBERRIES

CINNAMON MOCHA CREAM WITH TORTILLA CRISPS

COFFEE ALMOND ICE CREAM TORTE

COOKIE ICE CREAM-A-ROUNDS

CRANBERRIES 'N CREAM JUBILEE

GINGER PUMPKIN YOGURT PIE

HOLLY BERRY SUNDAE

LEMON RIBBON ICE CREAM PIE

MANGO SORBET WITH STRAWBERRY SAUCE

MOCHA HAZELNUT SYMPHONY

PEANUTTY ICE CREAM SANDWICHES

PINA COLADA PIE

PRALINE CREAM PUFFS

RASPBERRIES PEACHES 'N CREAM SHORTCAKE

REVEL BERRY ICE CREAM TORTE

4 | 5 | 6
The Scotch trade has thrived for decades on images of noble stags and club-room armchairs. Upstart drinks and changing tastes have begun to force a new attitude. Dewar's site plots a midway course, with lifestyle shots sitting on the warm and comforting cream of old. White Label, the flagship product, is recalled only in the page edges.

Dewar's promotes responsible drinking.
Dewar's, White Label and the Highlander Device are registered trademarks.
© 1999 Bacardi & Company Limited. Sole Distributor U.S. John Dewar & Sons Company, Miami, FL.
Blended scotch whisky - 40% Alc. by Vol.
<u>View our Privacy Statement</u>

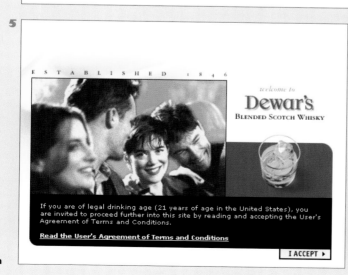

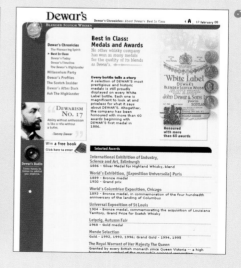

www.thefreedomtrail.org

4

INFORMATION BOOTH   FIRST STOP: REVOLUTION   ‹ EXPERIENCE THE TRAIL ›   THE FOUNDATION   GIFT SHOP

the freedom trail

In 1958, the City of Boston was changed in the subtlest of ways.

A red line was painted on the sidewalk, starting at the Boston Common and going downtown, to the North End, then over the bridge to Charlestown and up to the Bunker Hill monument.

Sixteen historic sites, all significant in this country's early struggle for freedom, were connected by a 2.5 mile stripe that not only linked one place to another, but the past to the present.

Here we continue The Freedom Trail's history by introducing its first official Web site. Have a look around. We hope it encourages you to come visit.

‹home›   contact us   guest book   credits

1 | 2 | 3 | 4

The cinema tradition is a great standby in the design of pages which are strongly photo-dependent. Colours appear more intense, there is an illusion of better image sharpness. The Old North Church screen successfully breaks the oft-stated rule of not using white running text against a black background.

5

www.coma2.com

6

7

8

9

5 | 6 | 7 | 8 | 9

The Web artists of the Coma² site should know what they're doing. This virtuoso production has all the signs of confidence. The red (standard FF0000), kicks out against the lined green background.

Confident in the audience too – the assumption is that the viewers will all be equipped with 24-bit colour. At lower resolutions, subtle shadow effects get minced by banding.

1

www.acornkitchens.com

3

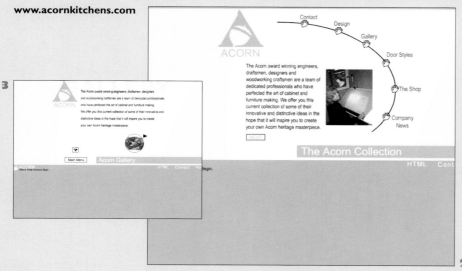

2

1 | 2 | 3

The shock of the weak! The Acorn site colour scheme is highly unusual, and appears to have taken inspiration from the desktop shot (2). Old folks with long memories will recall that almost all drawing boards came in that curious green, exactly half-way between restful and nauseating. A precariously clamped desk lamp lights the scene with a warm tungsten glow.

www.moet.com

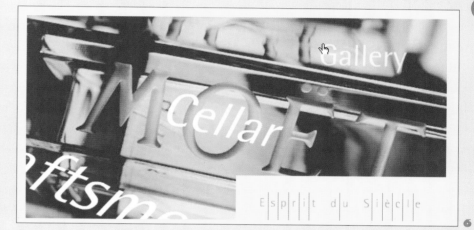

4 | 5 | 6 | 7

The Moët & Chandon site uses a virtually monochrome palette with the colours selected echoing 1930s photo chic. The wholemeal suite is deliberately chosen to hint at the taste of the product – a classic tasting note for champagne is 'biscuity'. The site contrasts with the public perception of a louder Moët & Chandon, familiar to us from thousands of Grand Prix motor-racing podia. Chromatic restraint and mannered type make all the difference here.

Thomas Feldmann

1

Inside the Agency
Portfolio
Awards
Services
Contact Us

More than you expect

Portfolio   [work] [select] © '99 | e-mail webmaster

2

Inside the Agency
Portfolio
Awards
Services
Contact Us

© '99 | e-mail webmaster   More than you expect.

Portfolio   (1) (2) (3) (4) (5) (6) (7) (8) (9) (10) (11) (12)

Teletron, Incorporated

Support Services Package

Folder and inserts
3 spot color/coated paper

Move your mouse cursor over the
thumbnails to see larger versions.

www.hirons.com

3

Inside the Agency

Portfolio

Awards

Services

Contact Us

© '99 | e-mail webmaster   More than you expect.

Portfolio

(1) (2) (3) (4) (5) (6) (7) (8) (9) (10) (11) (12)

IBM.
1999
校园招聘活动!

机遇就在眼前
欢迎积极参与

China Accounts

Client: IBM
Poster/2-color, coated paper

Client: Cummins
Bus brochure/4-color

Client: ASIMCO
Trade show handout/4-color

Move your mouse cursor over the
thumbnails to see larger versions.

1 | 2 | 3
In the Hirons Agency
site, an all-purpose
industrial grey sets
off a selection of
colourful illustrations.
The design rules are
those of traditional
corporate print – it's
not hard to imagine
these pages folded
neatly in half with a
wire stitch in the
middle.

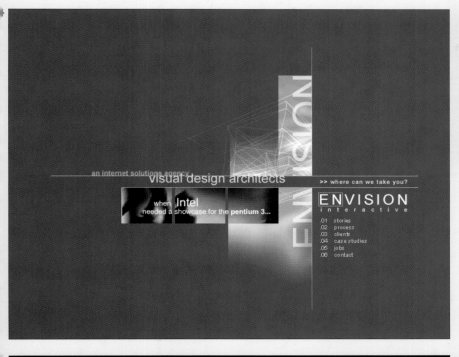

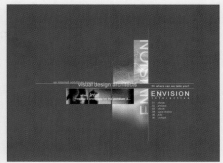

www.envisioninteractive.com

www.dennisinter.com

4 | 5 | 6 | 7

Two sites which stay in the strict confines of the monochrome palette, one with an airy photographic feel, the other sticking closely to street iconography. The Envision site (4, 5) stands up in low resolution, the soft graduations being inoffensively dithered (5). Dennis Interactive (6, 7) have no such concerns with a plain black ground and the benefit of the world's most well-known trouser tag. Finally, a question prompted by the Envision site: are Internet designers really architects? Or merely carpenters?

1

3

5

www.gabor.de

1 | 2 | 3 | 4 | 5

Skating deftly round some huge pitfalls, the Gabor site uses fancy footwork and a white background to make the screens look like familiar catalogue pages. Low depth-of-field photography gives a hint of what the 3-D Web might offer one day. The resulting feather-edged images blend seamlessly with the pervasive white ground. Elsewhere, the visual material retreats even further (*above*) to form a ground for the real business of the site – consumer personal data collection.

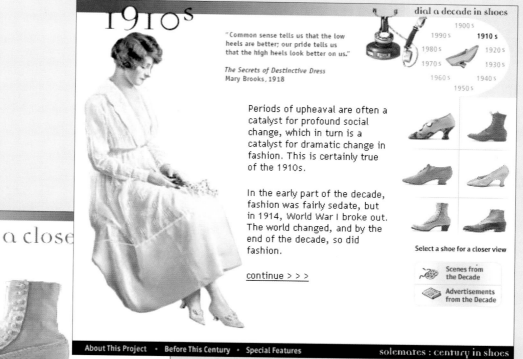

1910s

"Common sense tells us that the low heels are better; our pride tells us that the high heels look better on us."

The Secrets of Destinctive Dress
Mary Brooks, 1918

dial a decade in shoes

1900 s
1990 s   **1910 s**
1980 s   1920 s
1970 s   1930 s
1960 s   1940 s
1950 s

Periods of upheaval are often a catalyst for profound social change, which in turn is a catalyst for dramatic change in fashion. This is certainly true of the 1910s.

In the early part of the decade, fashion was fairly sedate, but in 1914, World War I broke out. The world changed, and by the end of the decade, so did fashion.

continue > > >

Select a shoe for a closer view

Scenes from the Decade

Advertisements from the Decade

About This Project • Before This Century • Special Features

solemates : century in shoes

1910s a close

zoom in

rotate   description

↑ ↓ ← → + −
Click on the shoe or use the buttons to zoom in and out.

close ●

www.centuryinshoes.com

6 | 7 | 8
In the Shoe History site's opening screen, the look of the 1910s is created using a limited-palette JPEG. This apparently monochrome image actually uses 21 different colours.

1910s a closer look

zoom in

rotate   description

↑ ↓ ← → + −
Click on the shoe or use the buttons to zoom in and out.

close ●

www.lego.com

80

1 | 2 | 3 | 4 | 5 | 6 | 7

Toy-box bright colours are the principal attraction to the Lego site. The Lego palette is extraordinarily well suited to the Web page. The addition of a few highlights lends an extra dimension to the screen and gives the feel of the toys themselves. The pages showing Lego's Star Wars merchandise (6, 7) employ the classic intergalactic background, a very economical GIF that is immediately recognizable.

8 | 9 | 10
The Cye personal robots site is aimed equally at children and adults, and so avoids the toy-box palette. The robot products forcibly influence the colours and shapes of every screen element. Next step – the robot Web-page designer?

www.personalrobots.com

1

www.aids.at

2

1 | 2 | 3

The Austrian AIDS site shows elegance and restraint, both in its use of colour and type. It neatly avoids the question of colour association by going monochrome.

There are many echoes here of the European tradition of political photo-montage, but brought up to date with a striking panoramic page format.

3

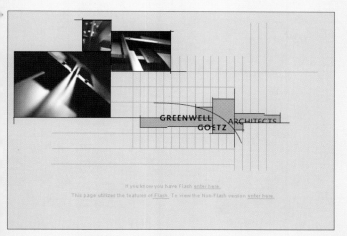

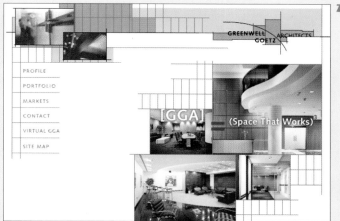

4 | 5 | 6 | 7 | 8

www.gga.com

Greenwell Goetz Architects opt for a bookish look, with solid colour used for the introductory 'chapter opener' pages and white ground for the subsequent text-rich pages. Blueprint colour photographs and 'hand-drawn' sketches add to the studious atmosphere.

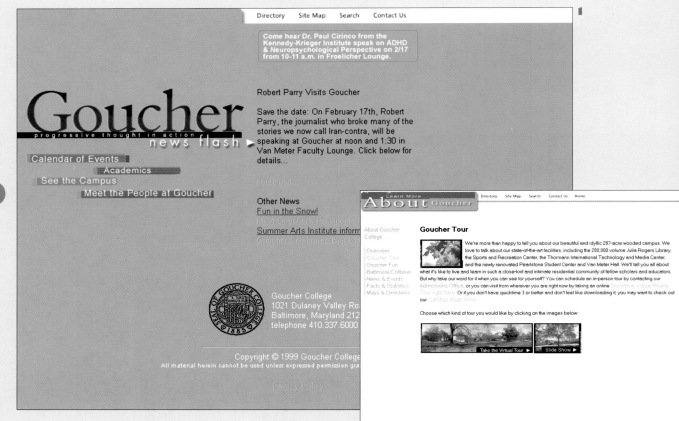

1 | 2 | 3

The Goucher and American Photography sites have very similar palettes. Both employ cool-blue backgrounds. The Goucher site has one additional blue and then starts to use green for text links and navigation; the text pages use black text against a white foreground. It has been deliberately made to look like a traditional college prospectus.

www.goucher.edu

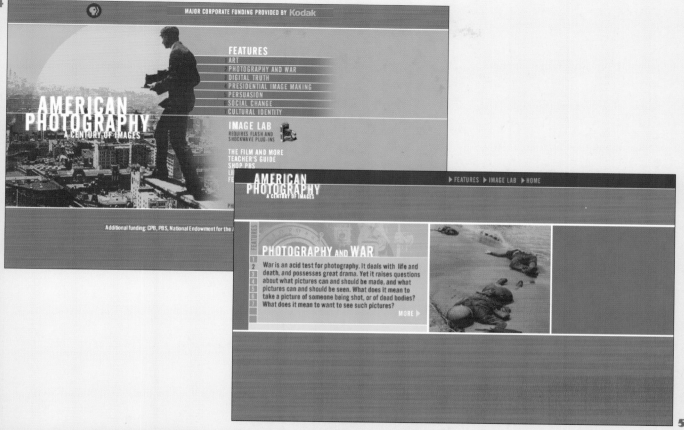

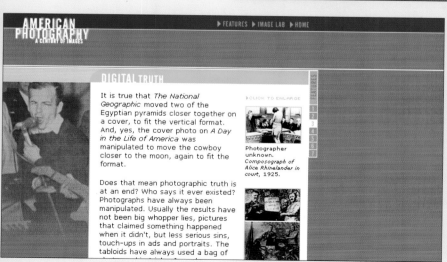

4 | 5 | 6

The prevailing style of 'serious' US Web design is well represented by the American Photography site. It is a guide to a television series produced by the Public Broadcasting Service. Powder blue and a highly contrasting orange are used in varying strengths to manage a multi-layer presentation. Extra values are gained by lavish use of horizontal 'scan lines' made of two colours. Served up as GIFs, these areas download at speed. The type hierarchy is also economically managed, using only combinations of blues and white.

www.pbs.org

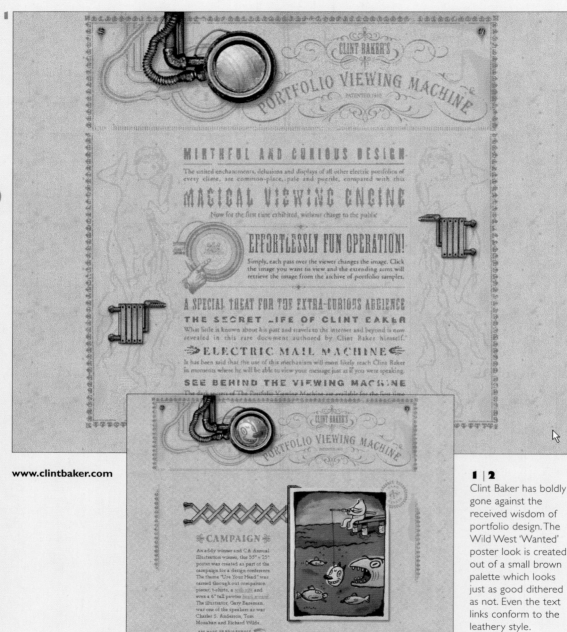

86

www.clintbaker.com

1 | 2
Clint Baker has boldly
gone against the
received wisdom of
portfolio design. The
Wild West 'Wanted'
poster look is created
out of a small brown
palette which looks
just as good dithered
as not. Even the text
links conform to the
leathery style.

3

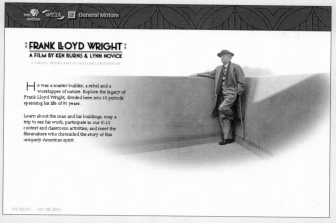

4

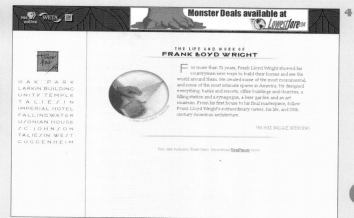

87

5

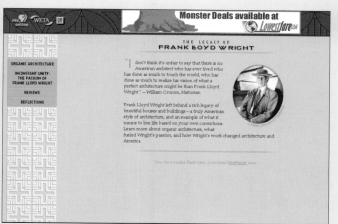

6

7

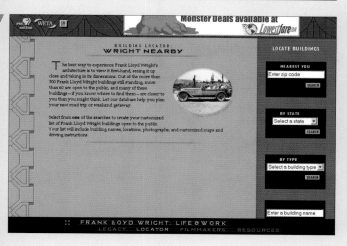

3 | 4 | 5 | 6 | 7

The Frank Lloyd Wright biography site is a *tour de force* of feather-edge-GIF management. You might think a limited palette has been used, but the actual number of colours is surprisingly high – several browns have been employed to produce subtle graduations of colour. The image stands up well to low resolution dithering (though the crass advertising banner threatens to undo all the good work).

www.pbs.org/flw

1

www.dataprotect.com

2

www.d2.com

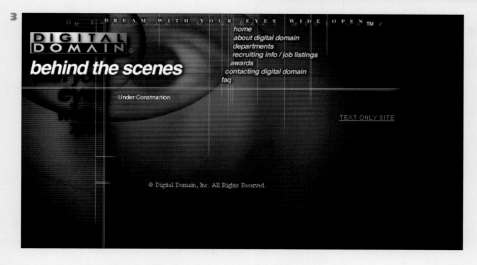

3

1 | 2

The Data Protect site is so subtle it is on the margins of invisibility. The illusion of monotone is given by a selection of very similar greens. The 'rubbed out' look which recurs throughout the site deserves a fuller description – manuscript writers, when short of virgin parchment, used to scrape away at a previously used sheet. The fibres generally resisted such abuse and retained a trace of the original scribing. The technical term for this is palimpsest.

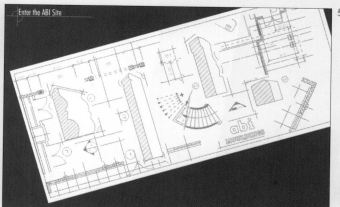

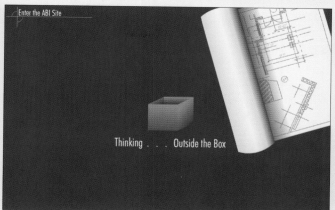

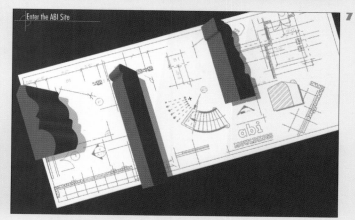

www.abimouldings.com

3 | 4 | 5 | 6 | 7 |

The Digital Domain site (*3*) opens on sombre background colours, the better to show off their bright, sparky digital film effects work. The site was still under construction at the time of writing. More dark colours are on display at the ABI Mouldings site (*4, 5, 6, 7*). This Flash-driven production has the moulded sections springing to animated life out of blueprints. The bronze logo adds a touch of warmth.

1 | 2 | 3
Nigel Holmes, the British grand old man of US information graphics, veteran of 16 years standing at *Time* magazine, launches himself upon the Web in primary colours. The junior school button icons demand to be clicked and reveal an impressive body of work in his inimitable style. It's a rare example of simple down-home graphics and cute drawing that actually works.

and down here, stuff about **lectures**

up there, you'll find **web graphics and animated charts** (not much, yet)

www.nigelholmes.com

4

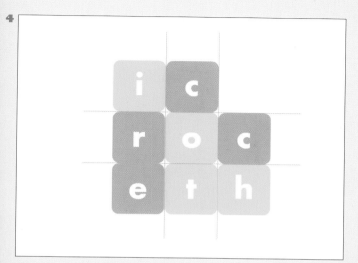

5

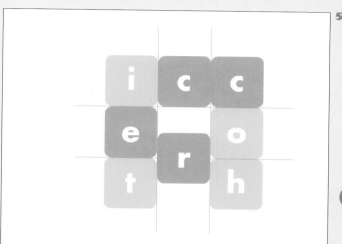

6

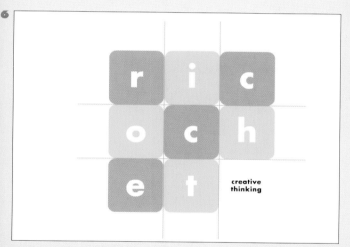

7

www.ricochetcreativethinking.ca

4 | 5 | 6 | 7
The Ricochet site works with Flash movies, and entices with an infuriatingly addictive version of the old sliding puzzle game. Powder blue and yellow are the colours of young, fresh, unfettered creative thinking. Well worth remembering.

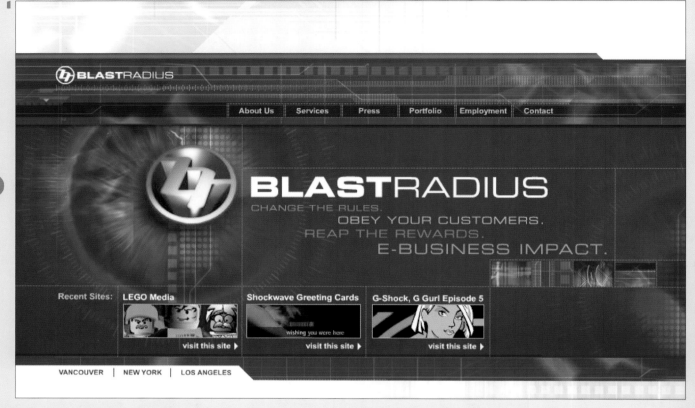

www.blastradius.com

1 | 2 | 3
Blastradius is a handy marker to symbolize Web design at the beginning of a new millennium. It is a synthesis of influences that stretch far back into science fiction magazines, futuristic literature and plain old mechanical fantasy. The blue light suffusing the scene is borrowed from any alien horror film of the 1960s, as are the trademark whirling vortices.

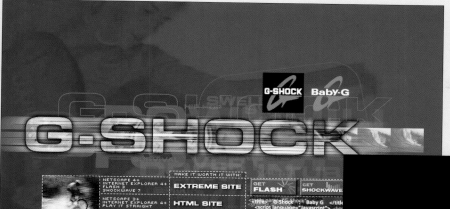

www.gshock.com

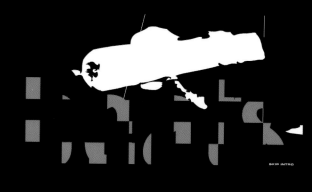

www.oneilleurope.com

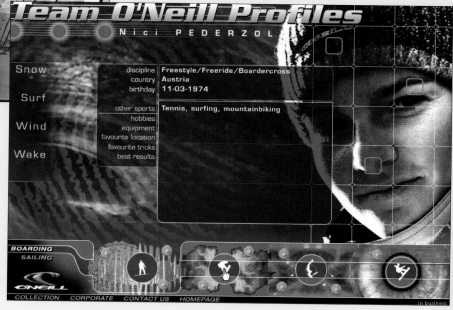

4 | 5 | 6 | 7
Designed by Blastradius (*opposite*) the G-Shock site (*4, 5*) comes in two versions – HTML and 'extreme'. The latter choice brings up a flash movie with none of the parent site's soft-edged qualities.

O'Neill (*6,7*) hits the spot for a boarding and sailing site: its blue, multi-layered and highly graduated. Self-awareness is neatly represented by the designer's sticky thumbprint at the foot of the screen.

94

Interior.
Black Cloth
Black Leather
Black Leatherette
Cream Cloth
Cream Leather
Cream Leatherette
Grey Cloth
Grey Leather
Grey Leatherette

Exterior.
Bright Blue
Green
Red
Dark Blue
White
Yellow
Black
Silver

Colors displayed may not all be available on your dealer's lot or for order from the factory at any given time.   Contact your dealer for current color availability.

Drivers wanted.

Interior.
Black Cloth
Black Leather
Black Leatherette
Cream Cloth
Cream Leather
Cream Leatherette
Grey Cloth
Grey Leather
Grey Leatherette

Exterior.
Bright Blue
Green
Red
Dark Blue
White
Yellow
Black
Silver

Colors displayed may not all be available on your dealer's lot or for order from the factory at any given time.   Contact your dealer for current color availability.

Drivers wanted.

www.turbonium.com

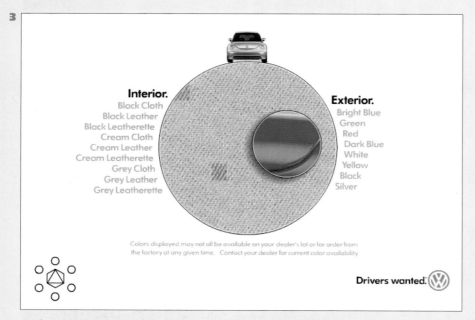

Interior.
Black Cloth
Black Leather
Black Leatherette
Cream Cloth
Cream Leather
Cream Leatherette
Grey Cloth
Grey Leather
Grey Leatherette

Exterior.
Bright Blue
Green
Red
Dark Blue
White
Yellow
Black
Silver

Colors displayed may not all be available on your dealer's lot or for order from the factory at any given time.   Contact your dealer for current color availability.

Drivers wanted.

1 | 2 | 3 | 4
The Volkswagen site has the look of traditional VW press advertising – a simple image of the car, a white ground and a pay-off strapline, all in the house futura face. Colour is the point here, and accurate colour at that. The viewer is able to test all the available paint and trim variations, choose features, and proceed all the way to just short of purchase. Some of the new Beetle colours are unusual so a dealer visit is advised to check the browser's view.

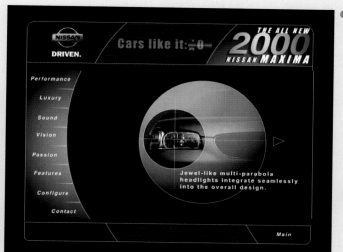

www.chryslercars.com

5 | 6 | 7 | 8 | 9

The Chrysler car (a 1930s retro wagon) is the hero. Black always made cars look good, and the profound black of a well-adjusted monitor makes them look even better. On this site as well you can try out vehicle colours – the browser takes a few moments to render the smart silver original into a rather less desirable Deep Cranberry Pearl Coat.

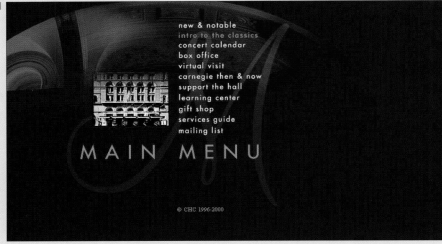

1 | 2 | 3
The Carnegie Hall site uses a colour combination straight out of the formal artist's wheel. A rich dark blue, evocative of luxury, pleasure and a concert hall atmosphere, is used for the background colour. This shows up the gold and red of the inset pictures vividly. The orange of the main text headings coordinates with the rollovers. A clean white background supports the text-heavy scroll of artists who have appeared at Carnegie Hall. James McNeill Whistler, who made a nocturne out of this very combination of colours, might be accorded a late entry into the Carnegie Hall of Fame.

www.carnegiehall.com

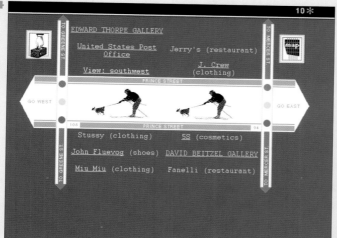

4 | 5 | 6 | 7

The New York SoHo site demonstrates the way of the new cartography. The names of the stores on West Broadway are plotted in the right geographical place; those with Web sites have clickable links. The choice of a dark green background forces a revision of the link colour conventions. Taking a cue from the traffic lights, life is red, style is yellow and art is green. Enterprises unequipped with links are relegated to the dullest of greys.

www.artseensoho.com

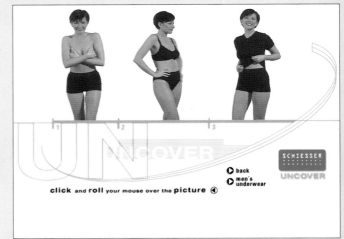

98

1 | 2 | 3 | 4

Power underwear was always going to be a tough brief, and this pitch by the Coma² agency makes a brave attempt. The microscopic token man in the opening screen, though clad in a monochrome mackintosh, is no deviant onlooker. Powered by QuickTime, he disrobes along with the girls. Flesh tones look good against a white ground, and blue has no sinister associations so the look is of a clean wholesome catalogue page.

www.coma2.com

5

6

7

8

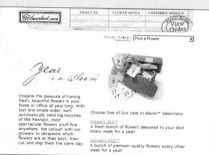

9

5 | 6 | 7 | 8 | 9

The flowerbud.com site offers a solution to any online florist's conundrum – the natural desire to show every flower in its true colours at life size is frustrated by the limitation of file size. Small colour images in well-judged colours draw the buyer in. The background with a faded-out green flower image is evocative of the palely printed wrapping paper traditionally used at the old-style florists' bench.

www.flowerbud.com

1 | 2 | 3 | 4

This Flash-driven site promoting the Ford installation moves along at a cracking pace. One of the virtues of the Flash application is that it encourages simpler and reductive design processes. Though the temptations of over-elaboration are still present, the demands of orchestrating animation as well as shape seem to lead to more elegant solutions. On the occasions where they don't, at least it's all over fairly quickly.

www.journey.ford.co.uk

101

5 | 6 | 7 | 8 | 9 | 10 | 11

The first five screens of the Cool Films site show an economy of both colour and style. But the black-and-white drawings are not only stylistically simple; they offer the simplest way of getting a moving image on screen. In the last two frames, reference is made to early pop videos. Screen (10) with its vibrant yellow border (waving a fond goodbye to naturalistic colour), owes a large debt to Jamie Reid's Sex Pistols artwork.

www.coolfilms.com

www.citibank.com

1 | 2
Deliberately styled like an online version of the corporate brochure, the Citibank site is fitted with simple rollovers which reveal selected sections in turn. The frieze graphics are in the tradition of the reassuringly naive style favoured by financial institutions to achieve the customer-friendly look. Warm colours liven the chosen topic – just remember that overdrafts were, are, and always will be red.

3

SITE ADMINISTRATION

Get fresh with your customers! Add new products, press releases, job openings and other information with Web Design Group's easy-to-use site administration system. It not only saves you money on maintenance, but it also keeps customers coming back to your site again and again. Plus, your employees can immediately update site information using a simple interface and an ordinary web browser like Netscape Navigator™ or Microsoft® Internet Explorer®. Now, keeping your web site accurate and up-to-date is as easy as point-and-click.

Clients Who Know

"Our web site is considered the latest source of property information for Prime Group's investors, tenants and prospective clients. Being able to immediately update and distribute company information ourselves using a simple browser gives us a huge advantage over our online competitors."

» Brandt Pfeifer
Dir. of Marketing
Prime Group Realty Trust

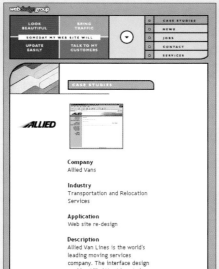

4

CASE STUDIES

Company
Allied Vans

Industry
Transportation and Relocation Services

Application
Web site re-design

Description
Allied Van Lines is the world's leading moving services company. The interface design enables Allied Van Lines to be

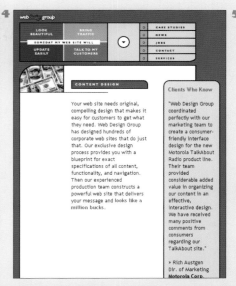

5

CONTENT DESIGN

Your web site needs original, compelling design that makes it easy for customers to get what they need. Web Design Group has designed hundreds of corporate web sites that do just that. Our exclusive design process provides you with a blueprint for exact specifications of all content, functionality, and navigation. Then our experienced production team constructs a powerful web site that delivers your message and looks like a million bucks.

Clients Who Know

"Web Design Group coordinated perfectly with our marketing team to create a consumer-friendly interface design for the new Motorola TalkAbout Radio product line. Their team provided considerable added value in organizing our content in an effective, interactive design. We have received many positive comments from consumers regarding our TalkAbout site."

» Rich Austgen
Dir. of Marketing
Motorola Corp.

103

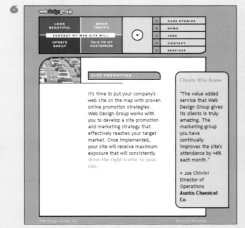

6

SITE PROMOTION

It's time to put your company's web site on the map with proven online promotion strategies. Web Design Group works with you to develop a site promotion and marketing strategy that effectively reaches your target market. Once implemented, your site will receive maximum exposure that will consistently drive the right traffic to your site.

Clients Who Know

"The value added service that Web Design Group gives its clients is truly amazing. The marketing group you have continually improves the site's attendance by +4% each month."

» Joe Chivini
Director of Operations
Austin Chemical Co.

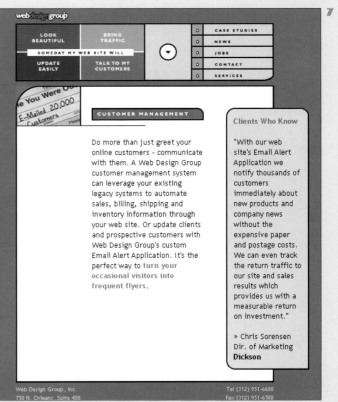

7

CUSTOMER MANAGEMENT

Do more than just greet your online customers - communicate with them. A Web Design Group customer management system can leverage your existing legacy systems to automate sales, billing, shipping and inventory information through your web site. Or update clients and prospective customers with Web Design Group's custom Email Alert Application. It's the perfect way to turn your occasional visitors into frequent flyers.

Clients Who Know

"With our web site's Email Alert Application we notify thousands of customers immediately about new products and company news without the expensive paper and postage costs. We can even track the return traffic to our site and sales results which provides us with a measurable return on investment."

» Chris Sorensen
Dir. of Marketing
Dickson

Web Design Group, Inc.
750 N. Orleans, Suite 400

Tel (312) 951-6688
Fax (312) 951-6588

3 | 4 | 5 | 6 | 7

Friendly style also at the Web Design Group. A simple logic – choose four colours and employ each one as a highlight colour in a dependent window.

The navigational device also unifies the text pages. The use of a themed colour graphic at the top left of each page adds interest to flat tints.

www.webdesigngroup.com

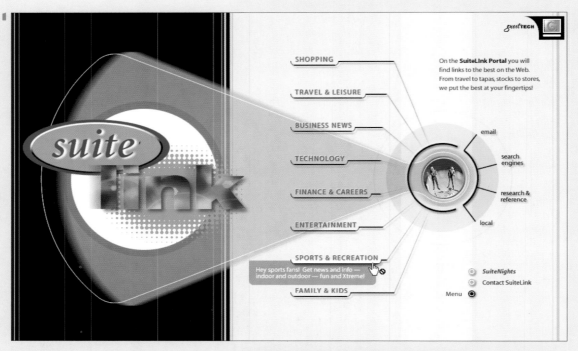

1 | 2 | 3
Image slicing gives a sophisticated 3-D appearance to Suite Link's opening page. A cornucopia of effects, such as white drop shadows, imitation halftone dot patterns and shadowed leader lines, is displayed in this screen. On subsequent pages the pastel background throws the 'Suite Link' logo into sharp relief. The transparency effect has been handled skilfully.

www.suitelink.com

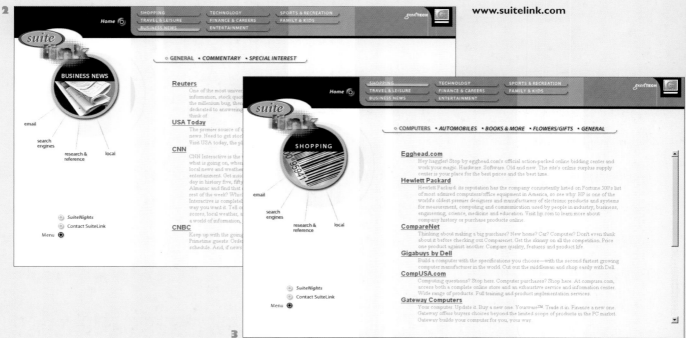

4 | 5 | 6
In the 'William B' site, top and bottom bands of deep pink draw attention with their brashness, making the bold statement that the clothes and design can stand up to the assault of deep pink. Less assured operators would retreat to the gloomier reaches of 'DimGray'.

Inspired by Fendi's handbags, this heavy cotton skirt has a silk trimmed waistband, full silk lining and **generous beaded fringe.**

Portobello Skirt

Welcome to williamb.com!

Check out the latest William B. styles by clicking on the roman numerals to the left.

Head back and click on any of the letters above to get the scoop on William B., find out our retail locations, get the skinny on who's wearing William B. and what the press is saying; and best of all, an exclusive sneak peak at what William B. is planning for next season.

Or you can always just play around with our fabulous color changer below.

Don't forget to e-mail us, join the William B. mailing list and tell us what you think of all this!

wb@williamb.com

105

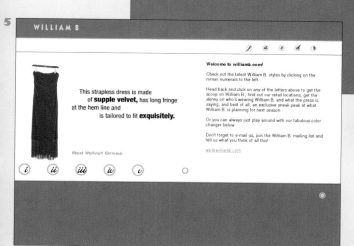

This strapless dress is made of **supple velvet,** has long fringe at the hem line and is tailored to fit **exquisitely.**

Red Velvet Dress

Welcome to williamb.com!

Check out the latest William B. styles by clicking on the roman numerals to the left.

Head back and click on any of the letters above to get the scoop on William B., find out our retail locations, get the skinny on who's wearing William B. and what the press is saying; and best of all, an exclusive sneak peak at what William B. is planning for next season.

Or you can always just play around with our fabulous color changer below.

Don't forget to e-mail us, join the William B. mailing list and tell us what you think of all this!

wb@williamb.com

www.williamb.com

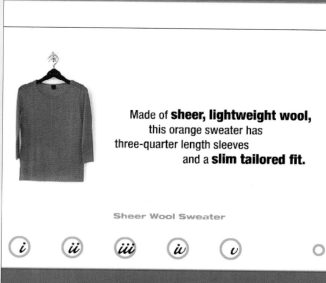

Made of **sheer, lightweight wool,** this orange sweater has three-quarter length sleeves and a **slim tailored fit.**

Sheer Wool Sweater

www.martini.com

1 | 2 | 3

Martini is riding high on the wave of 1970s retro chic. Strong bands of colours are set off by soft shades of grey. Looking nostalgically down into the colours of the cocktail glasses stimulates memories of ill-advised T-shirts. This largely wordless site encourages idle mouse-clicking on randomly presented images – just the thing for the happy hour.

4

www.independence-cigar.de

5

www.sfmoma.org

107

4 | 5
Further back, this
time, to the heights
of 1940s US military
chic with the
Independence Cigar
Company (4). The
blue-chinned pilot
epitomises the
fearless bravery of
flying and tobacco.
Pipe-smoking Belgian
René Magritte is
celebrated at the San
Francisco Museum of
Modern Art for his
1953 *Golconda* (5).
His description of the
process of picture-
making could stand
equally for Web-page
design: 'They evoke
mystery... when one
sees one of my
pictures, one asks
oneself the simple
question "What does
it mean?" – it does
not mean anything,
because mystery
means nothing either.
It is unknowable.'

www.southfloridatech.org

1 | 2
The pages from the South Florida Technical Data Organization demonstrate how to control texture and tone by the skilful manipulation of bands of colour in a limited palette. More elevated information heavy enterprises could learn from the understated clarity of this site.

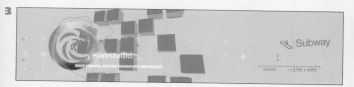

3

4

5

6

7

8

109

www.elixirstudio.com

9

3 | 4 | 5 | 6 | 7 | 8 | 9
The Elixir Studio site map deliberately looks like a metro map. Very self-referential, as this design group specializes in transport graphics. They have their fingers in other graphic pies as well, with machine images and violent colour contrast (3, 4).

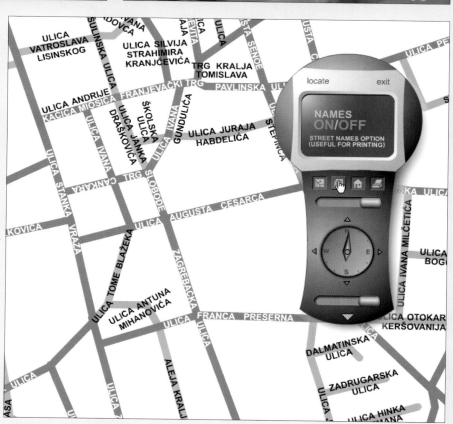

1

2

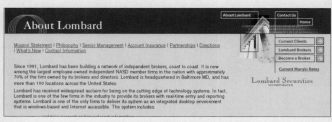

www.golombard.com

3

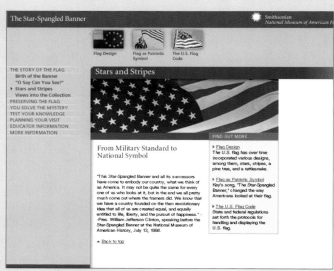

4

5

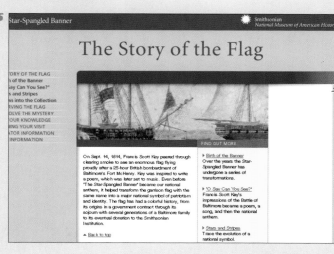

1 | 2 | 3 | 4 | 5 | 6 | 7 | 8

The green ('dark khaki') background selected for these sites is rarely seen in print – it is rather muddy and difficult to render attractively. On the Web, however, it has come to denote scholarship and wholesomeness (lots of museum sites use it). The Walrus site (6, 7, 8) makes great use of this potentially mucky end of the spectrum, with a cheerful yellow for emphasis.

www.americanhistory.si.edu

6

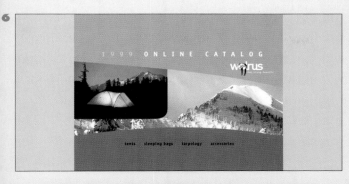

1999 ONLINE CATALOG

walrus
fast, strong, beautiful

tents   sleeping bags   tarpology   accessories

8

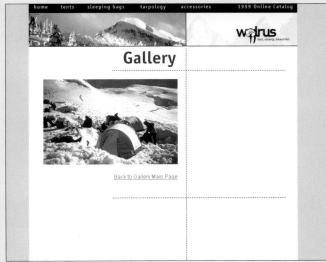

home   tents   sleeping bags   tarpology   accessories   1999 Online Catalog

walrus
fast, strong, beautiful

Gallery

Back to Gallery Main Page

www.walrusgear.com

home   tents   sleeping bags   tarpology   accessories   1999 Online Catalog

CLICK HERE ▶ | 4 Season Technical
| Backpacker
| Active Family

walrus
fast, strong, beautiful

POLE SLEEVES

SEAM-TAPING

GROMMETS

QUIET ZIPPER PULLS

QUIET ZIPPER PULLS
Our quiet zipper pulls of braided cord and plastic tabs that are large and easy to use - even with gloves on.

QUIET ZIPPER PULLS

GROMMETS

GROMMETS
Made in the U.S. out of solid brass, our spur grommets are as tough as they get. With multiple grommets on each strap you are guaranteed a tight pitch.

Go ahead and keep your expectations high.

You expect a lot when you buy a tent - and you should. We design and build our tents with the assumption that you demand the best possible design, materials and functionality that you can find in a tent. Then we make them affordable. So, whether you are looking for extra storage to keep your gear dry, or storm worthiness to keep you dry, you are going to find Walrus meets your needs - all at a cost that won't bleed your wallet dry.

▶ TENT FINDER

THE TENT
While the flysheet is the roof over your head, the tent body is your living room. You want your living room to be nice and dry, with no intrusive insects, and your tent should be too. With a Walrus there is room to store things, room to fully sit up*, lie down easily to sleep or to stargaze, and the ability to control ventilation. The basic comforts are always there in a Walrus tent.

* the ultra-light series may not accommodate sitting up

VENTILATION
Our large doors, expansive windows and strategically placed "eyelid" vents insure maximum airflow for the ultimate control in ventilation.

VENTILATION

VESTIBULES

VESTIBULES
Large and well-ventilated, our pole-supported vestibules offer extra protection from the elements.

CONTROLLABLE VENTS
Our new "eyelid" vents increase your control over tent ventilation.

CONTROLLABLE VENTS

FIELD REPAIRABLE POLES
Our tent poles are some of the strongest in the industry - Extruded from 7001 Hi-tensule aluminum, our poles are anodized for protection from the elements. The shock-corded, locking tip assures a secure connection for a tightly pitched tent. With a pole this strong it is easy to understand how we can guarantee them for life.

▶ FIELD REPAIRABLE POLES

FLYSHEETS
Our rainflys are made of an exclusive blend of polyester and nylon, in a weave we call Diamondback™. This combination resists UV degradation better than nylon alone, and is more dimensionally stable, providing less sag when wet and less shrinkage when hot. Flysheets are cut to fully protect the tent by coming down low to the ground, while leaving space for airflow to come up and under the fly, helping prevent condensation build-up. Set-up is a breeze with guypoints that attach to the tent frame, and easy to use side-release buckles that fasten to the treated, non-wicking, stake-out webbing. Care is taken to pattern and cut the rainfly, so it will taut to quickly shed rain.

GEARLOFTS & STORAGE POCKETS
We've all scrambled to find our flashlight under the seas of sleeping bags and gear in our tent, but with our handy and unobtrusive gear lofts and storage pockets, everything will be in easy reach.

112

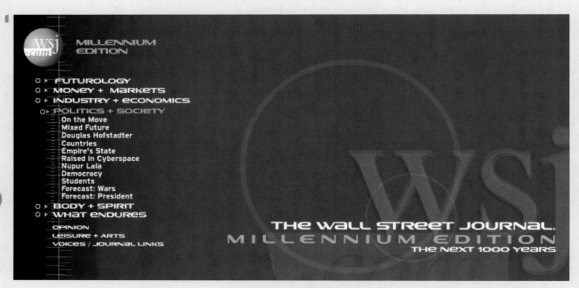

1

The Wall Street Journal has long had a strong presence on the Internet. Drop shadows here give a 'carved in stone' effect – suitable for a paper that firmly believes it will be around for the next 1,000 years. The broad graduated background, however, gets badly dithered in low-end browsers.

interactive.wsj.com

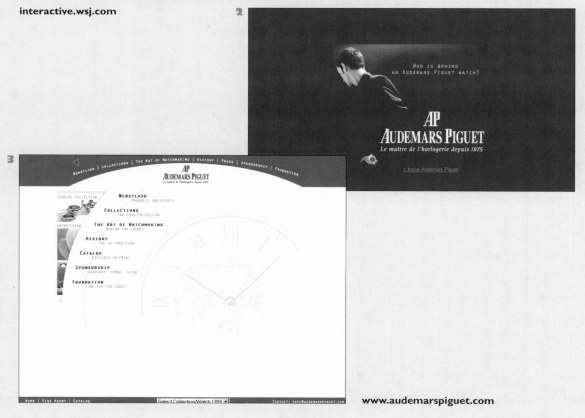

2 | 3

The Audemars Piguet opening screen benefits from assured image control in the way the background colour has invaded the central image. The dominant green colour is picked up in the background of the subsequent screen.

www.audemarspiguet.com

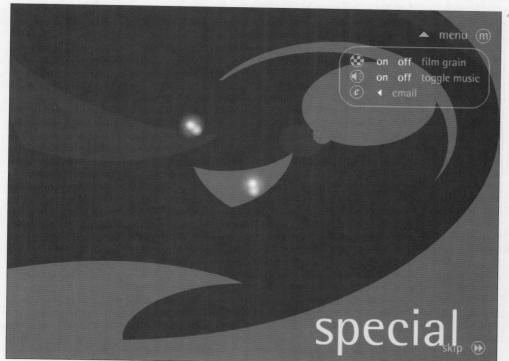

4

4 | 5
This site shows the
use of two close
colours to create
witty illusion. Which is
the figure and which
is the ground? They
appear to change
places seamlessly.

113

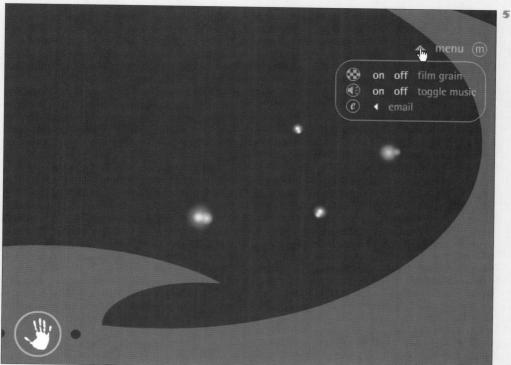

5

114

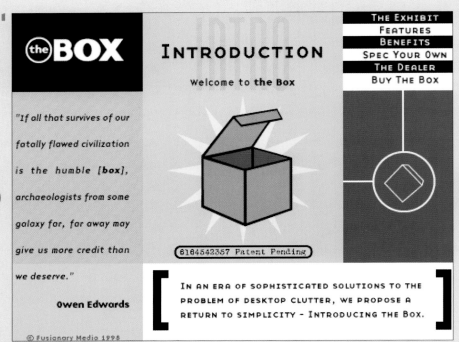

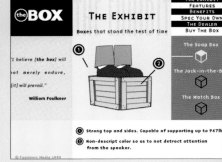

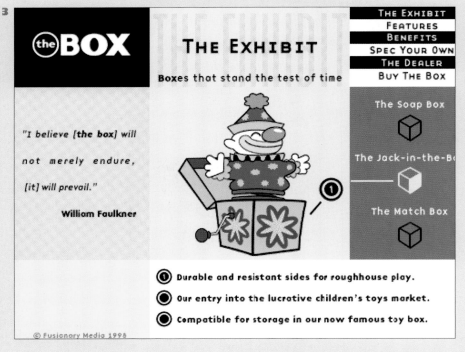

1|2|3|4|5|6|7|8|9

An object lesson in gaining attention and memorability through the use of colour and contrast. The format remains consistent across the whole site; only the colour blocks change. Three colours are used on each page, along with black and white; and the colours selected are shades of each other. Note the subliminal repetition of the page title on the background of the central panel, in the 'midtone' of the three colours selected. You may hate it, the box as well as the T-shirt, but you'll never forget it.

www.sixsides.com

Panel 4

the BOX

BENEFITS
Why you should own **the Box**

THE EXHIBIT
FEATURES
BENEFITS
SPEC YOUR OWN
THE DEALER
BUY THE BOX

"Dost thou love life? Then do not squander [the box], for that is the stuff life is made of."

Benjamin Franklin

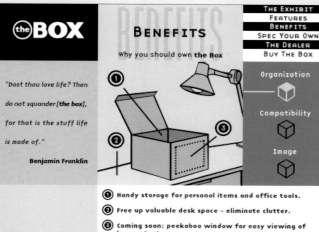

Organization

Compatibility

Image

① Handy storage for personal items and office tools.
② Free up valuable desk space – eliminate clutter.
③ Coming soon: peekaboo window for easy viewing of box contents.

Panel 5

the BOX

THE DEALER
Your exclusive source for **the Box**

THE EXHIBIT
FEATURES
BENEFITS
SPEC YOUR OWN
THE DEALER
BUY THE BOX

"The measure of a man is what he does with [the box]."

Pittacus

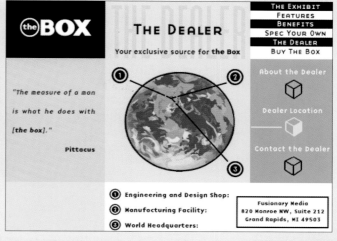

About the Dealer

Dealer Location

Contact the Dealer

① Engineering and Design Shop:
② Manufacturing Facility:
③ World Headquarters:

Fusionary Media
820 Monroe NW, Suite 212
Grand Rapids, MI 49503

Panel 6

the BOX

BENEFITS
Why you should own **the Box**

THE EXHIBIT
FEATURES
BENEFITS
SPEC YOUR OWN
THE DEALER
BUY THE BOX

"Dost thou love life? Then do not squander [the box], for that is the stuff life is made of."

Benjamin Franklin

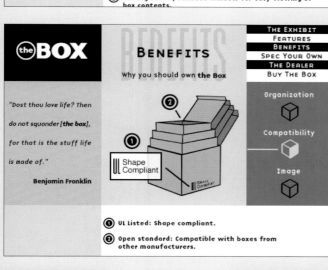

Organization

Compatibility

Image

① UL Listed: Shape compliant.
② Open standard: Compatible with boxes from other manufacturers.

Panel 7

the BOX

BUY THE BOX
Become a proud owner of **the Box**

THE EXHIBIT
FEATURES
BENEFITS
SPEC YOUR OWN
THE DEALER
BUY THE BOX

"There are only two truly infinite things, the universe and [the box]. And I am unsure about the universe."

Albert Einstein

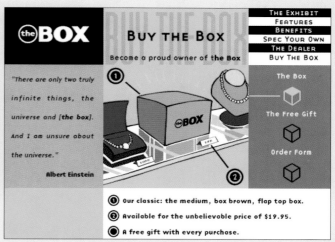

The Box

The Free Gift

Order Form

① Our classic: the medium, box brown, flap top box.
② Available for the unbelievable price of $19.95.
③ A free gift with every purchase.

Panel 8

the BOX

THE DEALER
Your exclusive source for **the Box**

THE EXHIBIT
FEATURES
BENEFITS
SPEC YOUR OWN
THE DEALER
BUY THE BOX

"The measure of a man is what he does with [the box]."

Pittacus

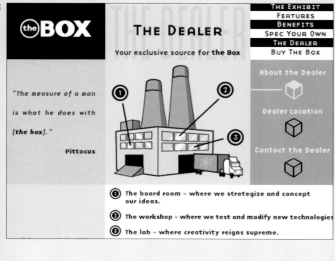

About the Dealer

Dealer Location

Contact the Dealer

① The board room – where we strategize and concept our ideas.
② The workshop – where we test and modify new technologies.
③ The lab – where creativity reigns supreme.

Panel 9

the BOX

BUY THE BOX
Become a proud owner of **the Box**

THE EXHIBIT
FEATURES
BENEFITS
SPEC YOUR OWN
THE DEALER
BUY THE BOX

"There are only two truly infinite things, the universe and [the box]. And I am unsure about the universe."

Albert Einstein

◄ FRONT

BACK ►

Colors

The Box

The Free Gift

Order Form

① Easy access holes for neck and arms.
② Pseudo quote courtesy of Albert Einstein.
③ Roomy fit, short-sleeved, 100% cotton, Beefy-T.

1

Welcome to our website.
Check out our 1999 science fair winners!
Award in Biodiversity Conservation Science

Investigate Biodiversity. An on-line toolbox to research global biodiversity -- the plants, animals, and other organisms living on the planet Earth.

Investigate Biodiversity

⊕ BIODIVERSITY MATTERS! ⊕ THREATS ⊕ CONSERVATION WORKS! ⊕ EXPLORE AND DISCOVER ⊕ RESOURCE POOL

For the Life of the Planet!

CONSERVATION INTERNATIONAL   int_el

read about the CI-INTEL Collaboration

© 1999 Conservation International Foundation, Washington, DC, Legal Notice.
Questions or comments, contact: webmaster@conservation.org.

developed by **gr8**

1 | 2 | 3
In the Biodiversity site strong nature colours have, appropriately, been chosen. The green suggests plant life; the blue suggests water; and the yellow, sunshine. Additional strong colours, such as purple, red and orange are used in the headers and navigation bars.

2

Investigate Biodiversity

⊕ BIODIVERSITY MATTERS! ⊕ THREATS ⊕ CONSERVATION WORKS! ⊕ EXPLORE AND DISCOVER ⊕ RESOURCE POOL

Collecting Data
1 2 3 4
5 6 7 8   **5**

Collecting Data ▪

Now that you've planned your study and developed a research question or hypothesis, you can start collecting data. This is where the fun really begins! There are three principal ways to collect data in biodiversity research. You can use any or all of these methods, depending on the objectives of your study. Clearly defined objectives will help you decide what type of data you need and how to collect it.

Field Sampling
The traditional way to collect data on biodiversity is to do field sampling. This involves going out into the field and physically collecting the data. The "field" can be any place where you're likely to find biodiversity. As you can imagine, this is almost everywhere on earth! There are some places that are inherently more interesting than others, and it's up to you to decide what aspects of biodiversity are interesting to you.

Remote Sensing
A second type of data collection is remote sensing, which refers to data collected from satellites orbiting the earth or cameras mounted on the wings of airplanes. Satellite images of the earth's surface are valuable to conservation biologists studying large areas. Aerial photography and videography provide scientists with images of particular areas. The data that are collected come in the form of satellite images, photographs, and video. These images are particularly important in helping to detect environmental changes in ecosystems over extended periods of time. They also enable scientists to study much larger areas than are feasible with traditional field methods.

Analyzing Existing Datasets
A third option is to gather data that other people have collected (with their permission, of course) and analyze it in a different way. This is a very good option if you are interested in a part of the world that you can't get to yourself, or if you want to compare the data that you collect with data from other parts of the world. Using existing data sets can be just as challenging as collecting and analyzing your own data.

Biodiversity Matters I Threats I Conservation Works I Explore and Discover I Resource Pool I Home

© 1999 Conservation International Foundation, Washington, DC, Legal Notice.

CONSERVATION   int_el

┌ Navigation Pathway ┐
▪ The Research Question
▪ Generating a Hypothesis
▪ Designing a Research Study
▪ Writing Your Proposal
▪ Collecting Data
▪▪ Field Sampling
▪ Analyzing Data
▪ Drawing Conclusions
▪ Research Proposals
▪ Taking Action

Site Tools
Select One ▼   go

www.clients.gr8.com

3

Investigate Biodiversity

⊕ BIODIVERSITY MATTERS! ⊕ THREATS ⊕ CONSERVATION WORKS! ⊕ EXPLORE AND DISCOVER ⊕ RESOURCE POOL

EXPLORE AND DISCOVER

Forming a Research Question
Generating a Hypothesis
Designing a Research Study
Writing Your Proposal
Collecting Data
Analyzing Data
Drawing Conclusions
Presenting and Writing Results
Taking Action

► References   ► Links

Hey! It Could Be a New Species!

Doing research on biodiversity is exciting. It's also extremely important. Time is running out for many of the species and communities that share the planet with us. We need good science to back up our conservation strategies, and there are too few conservation biologists, especially in tropical countries, to tackle the huge problem of biodiversity loss. We need innovative thinkers and solutions.

Exploring ecosystems and collecting data are a big part of biodiversity research, whether you're in a rain forest, desert, tundra, or prairie. You can study large-scale patterns in biodiversity and how they change over time using remotely sensed data (such as satellite imagery). You can analyze other people's data in new ways by asking different questions or compare their data to your own. How you make sense of your data is the essential next step.

As with any other scientific pursuit, a systematic approach to researching biodiversity is essential. By following the scientific method, you can break your research down into manageable pieces. It will help you ask the right scientific questions and ensure that you end up with valid conclusions. This section is a guide to helping you do research on biodiversity. Let's get started!

The Thrill of the Chase

Site Tools go
Select One ▼

4 | 5 | 6
In the Sylvan School site, conservative dark and royal blues suggest tradition and stability, while the gold is the gilt of achievement.

4

5

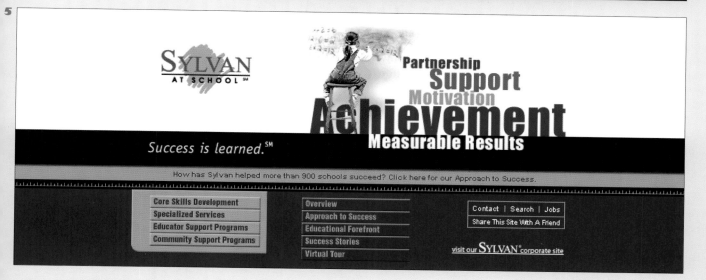

www.sylvanatschool.com

6

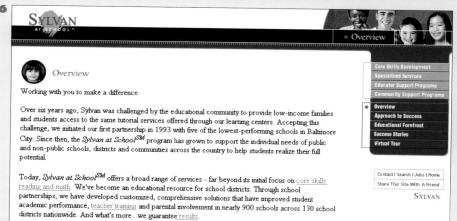

118

1 | 2 | 3 | 4 | 5 | 6

These three sites demonstrate how subtle pastels and curved shapes on a white background can create a subtle effect. Aptly, for the Photographers site (*1, 2, 3*) the conceit is to use icons from conventional print for authentication purposes. Registration marks, tint and colour bars, and typographical construction lines have all been used for adornment. The look of a grid sheet on the opening screen takes this a stage further. The Meteorit site (*6*) is high-key, elegant and multi-layered, and equally garnished with

www.photographers.de

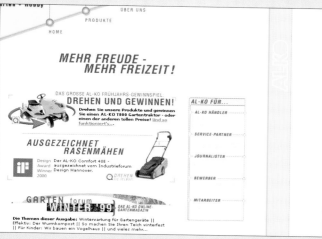

www.al-ko.com

construction lines. Alko (4, 5) are in the unglamorous business of making trailer hitches and caravan chassis, with lawn-mower manufacture for light relief. They have chosen white for the ground with red for emphasis.

www.coma2.com

1

www.maxwelllive.com

2

www.jenniferlopez.com

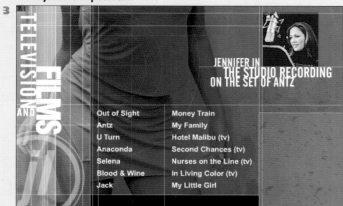

3

www.jewel-web.com

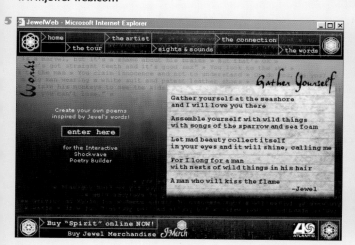

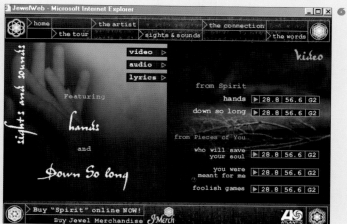

1 | 2 | 3 | 4 | 5 | 6 | 7

These screens all demonstrate the use of the duotone image. The Maxwell site (1) features underwater graphics and the turquoise colours of tropical waters, but nobody looks good in that shade of green. The Jennifer Lopez site (2, 3), on the other hand, shows off the economy of style that record-sleeve designers are expert at. The site designers have placed a visual pun on the screens: Web design is a rectangular activity, and self-referential construction lines have been left onsite. The well-judged reds and browns are complemented by the pale blue. The Jewel site (4, 5, 6, 7) offers a variety of duotone mood shades alongside busy design, and a script typeface to add atmosphere.

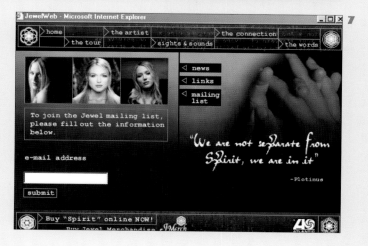

122

www.ldg.be

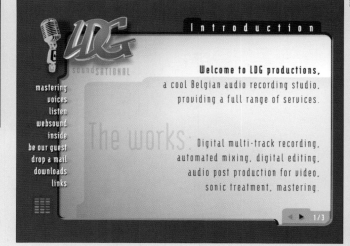

1 | 2 | 3

The unifying theme of the sites on these two pages is the cinema. In their different ways, each is concerned with evoking the movies or going to the movies.

The LDG site uses three reds to create a plush effect, recalling red-velvet curtains and old-fashioned cinema seats. This cinema-going theme hangs together with

the silvery grey of the wide text area – the red-plush curtains having opened to reveal the 'silver screen'.

www.hollywoodpartners.de

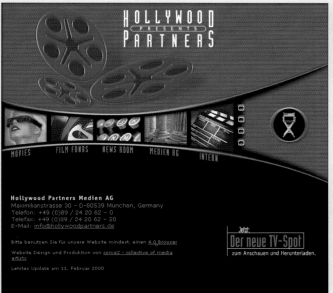

Hollywood Partners Medien AG
Maximilianstrasse 30 - D-80539 München, Germany
Telefon: +49 (0)89 / 24 20 62 - 0
Telefax: +49 (0)89 / 24 20 62 - 20
E-Mail: info@hollywoodpartners.de

Bitte benutzen Sie für unsere Website mindest. einen 4.0 Browser

Website Design und Produktion von coma2 - collective of media artists

Letztes Update am 11. Februar 2000

www.hitchcock100.com

4 | 5 | 6 | 7
Hollywood Partners (4, 5) love films, and the more cinematic the film, the more they love them. In the swooping three-colour drive-by home page there are small-screen tricks to savour; the translucent film reels, type distortion which follows the curves of the page, and an unusual attention to detail in the stylish edge finish round the top of the page. Universal Studios (6, 7) celebrate the centenary of Alfred Hitchcock's birth in high contrast horror style. The correctly adjusted monitor will show monochrome – try turning up the green for a satisfyingly ghoulish effect.

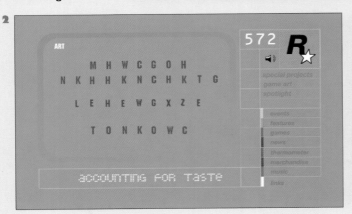

ROCKSTAR **NEWS**

143

Loading

news archive
view by type

events
features
games
thermometer
merchandise
music
art
links

www.rockstargames.com

ART

M H W C G O H
N K H H K N C H K T G
L E H E W G X Z E
T O N K O W C

572

special projects
game art
spotlight

events
features
games
news
thermometer
merchandise
music
links

accounting for taste

ART
SPECIAL PROJECTS

ARTIST,
TITLE,
TITLE OF PIECE:
PAGE:

143

game art
spotlight

events
features
games
news
thermometer
merchandise
music
links

accounting for taste

1 | 2 | 3 | 4 | 5 | 6 | 7

These screens all
show the use of
strong, bright back-
ground colours with
limited text and
image in the fore-
ground. They grab
attention with their

simplicity and
boldness. Rockstar
News (1, 2, 3) is
unafraid to use neon
green, although the
brightness of the
background is
mitigated to some

extent by a darker,
more moderate
green. Flat colour and
Flash drive Formitas –
a Slovenian marketing
and PR site (5, 6, 7).
After the moiré
wheel has done its

turn, skill is required
to chase and click on
your chosen topic as
it rotates at a brisk
pace; more well-
selected colours
follow, giving the site
a classy modern look.

The Züritel site (4)
follows the same
basic principle, though
a contrasting blue has
been added to the
rich orange ground
to pick out the
company's name.

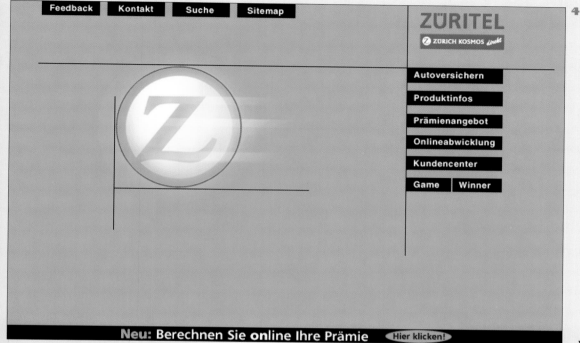

4

125

www.zuritel.ch

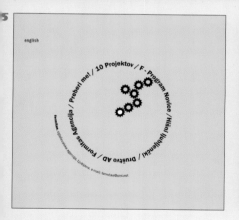

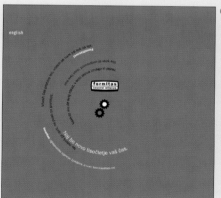

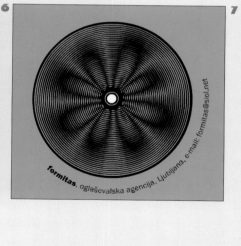

5

6

7

www.formitas.si

1

View projects

Webdesign

PRINTED MEDIA   WEBDESIGN   TYPEDESIGN   CD-ROMS

Conception and creation of
custom-made Internet presentations
and redesign of existing pages.
Inclusive HTML programming,
Shockwave Flash + Director,
JavaScript, Dynamic HTML etc..

PHILOSOPHY

CONTACT

2

http://www.vdnord.de

We have created
the screendesign
for the web
presentation of
VDN (a german
federation for
print industry
and new media),
in association
with City Vox,
Hamburg.

1 2 3 4 5 6 7 8 9 10 >

Back

http://www.schlaflos.com

You have seen the new
film with Meg Ryan and
Tom Hanks?

Well, this is life:
chat, mail, find friends
via internet and have
fun...

We have realized this
Flash/HTML site for
an agency in Hamburg,
Germany.

1 2 3 4 5 6 7 8 9 10 >

Back

www.rullkoetter.de

1 | 2 | 3 | 4 | 5 | 6
The look of both
these sites is sombre;
though unrelated,
they have strong
design similarities
which have their
roots in print. An
enthusiasm for
calligraphic type
forms is evident,
but it's the expert
management of small
graduations of black
that distinguishes
these sites from
the usual crowd.

4

Impressum

Produziert von
DER POOL - Team für Werbung, Rothenbaumchaussee 193-195, 20149 Hamburg
Telefon (o 40) 41 46 47-0, Telefax (o 40) 44 43 22, e-mail: info@der-pool.de

Konzept, Design & Umsetzung
Dirk Rullkötter AGD (Werbung + Design), Kleines Heenfeld 19, 32278 Kirchlengern
Telefon (o 52 23) 7 34 90, Telefax (o 52 23) 76 02 30, e-mail: info@rullkoetter.iok.net
http://www.rullkoetter.iok.net

Audio-Postproduction („Eulentraum" © toi, toi, toi Records 1998)
Studio Funk KG Hamburg (Berlin, Düsseldorf, Frankfurt am Main),
ussee 69, 20259 Hamburg,
32 04-3, Telefax (o 40) 4 32 04-500, e-mail: info@studiofunk.de

Die Aktion
Schirmherrschaft
Das Gemälde
Jugendwerk
Förderkreis
Glasaktie
Der Künstler

127

Der Künstler

Die Aktion
Schirmherrschaft
Das Gemälde
Jugendwerk
Förderkreis
Glasaktie
Der Künstler

Impressum

www.schatten.de

6

Die Aktion
Schirmherrschaft
Das Gemälde
Jugendwerk
Förderkreis
Glasaktie
Der Künstler

Impressum

Eine Aktion des „Förderkreis zugunsten Jugendwerk"

www.fscard.co.uk

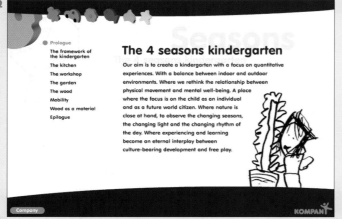

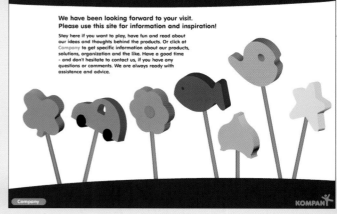

www.kompan.com

1 | 2 | 3

Marbles (*1*) are a charge card company. Its look represents a welcome and significant change in the working methods of the brand development industry – from the designer's perspective at least. In a market now terribly short of words to imply success, financial probity and status, the trend is to visual whimsy. Hundreds of such cards offer the same service, but maybe the playground memory of marbles is enough to distinguish this one from the crowd. In the world of real children, playground equipment makers Kompan (*2, 3*) make do with rubber fish.

www.woodblock.simplenet.com

4 | 5 | 6
In San Francisco, Kha Hoang professes himself to be a naughty child with a petulant opening message and climbing-frame graphics.

www.movedesign.com

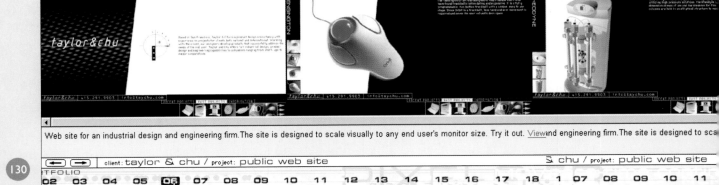

Web site for an industrial design and engineering firm. The site is designed to scale visually to any end user's monitor size. Try it out. View and engineering firm. The site is designed to scal

client: taylor & chu / project: public web site

www.mollysyes.com

1 | 2 | 3

Move Design (*1*) offer an interesting angle on the problem of scaling any viewer's monitor resolution. Visit the site for a demonstration but be prepared for an immediate and lengthy Shockwave player download. Mollys Yes (*2, 3*) follow the simpler rock band tradition of letter-box shaped windows. Move Design are fond of their blue trackball; the band have an affection for their green sound level meter.

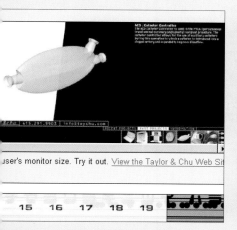

user's monitor size. Try it out. View the Taylor & Chu Web Si

15 16 17 18 19

www.ecco.com

4 | 5 | 6 | 7

Those suffering from bad feet can luxuriate in the soothing balm of the Ecco shoes site, while aspiring to own such costly but life-enhancing footwear. Layers of pastel blue in the background image are picked up in the navigation bars and make an effective foil for the red link buttons.

132

1

Please move your mouse over the timeline
to get more information.

Setting up of clean-rooms within
production departments.

1947   1967   1978   1988

1 2 3

www.buenderglas.com

2

bg p bünder glas gmbh plastoform

Intelligent Solutions for Pharmaceutics & Medical Technology

Portrait   Career   A company of the
Quality & Technology   Info Service   GERRESHEIMER group
Products   Contact
News   Links

                  Editor   Deutsch English

www.wyland.com

3

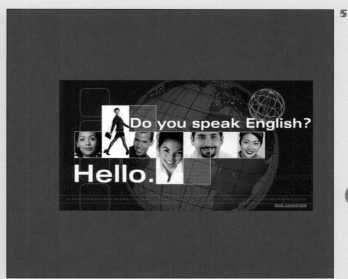

1 | 2 | 3 | 4 | 5 | 6 | 7

Bünder Glas (*1, 2*) uses petrol blue with a lighter version of the same blue in a duotone-photo effect. The same lighter blue in shadow lettering adds an extra layer of texture. The strapline and corporate logo is in reversed-out white lettering, while the main text area has a white ground with petrol-blue lettering. A small amount of yellow appears in the icons. The Wyland site (*3*) shows the same basic colour struct-ure, but uses three blues with a contrasting yellow to highlight. Reversed-out white lettering is also used on the Wall Street Institute site (*4, 5, 6, 7*). British readers will not be surprised to see the English language promoted in red, white and blue, but it is clear from the logo and style that this is the US version.

www.wallstreetinstitute.com

134

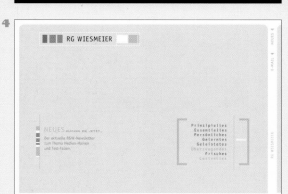

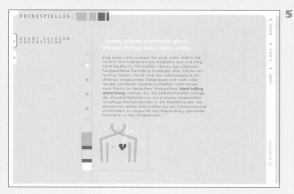

www.wiesmeier.de

1 | 2 | 3 | 4 | 5
International outfit Oven Digital (*1, 2, 3*) opt for a colour solution that emphasizes their portfolio shots, while their own corporate image recedes into the background. Grey screens are garnished with yellow prompts throughout with GIF type (no HTML anywhere) in only grey, black or white. German advertising agency Wiesmeier (*4, 5*) is even more recessive, with light-cream and pale-grey in profusion. Even the background piano music is hyper-discreet. A little colour is allowed on a subsequent screen (*5*), and even a punning reference to hard/heart selling.

3 www.ovendigital.com

6 | 7 | 8

Pos IT are market leaders in Web design in Tasmania, and their site shows that although design on the Web knows no boundaries, there are variations which must be due to local experience. Who *is* that guy?

http://www.posit.com.au

information technology

positive

6

8

Sun Netra Range
DTS
Ascend
Cisco
Aironet
Netscape

...sIT have reseller arrangements with ...ese companies and also use and ...commend their products.

products

positive

communications

about us
clients
products
services
contact
home

...osIT have been acknowledged by ...ese clients as their preferred Internet and New Media production house.

clients

information technology

positive

www.posit.com.au

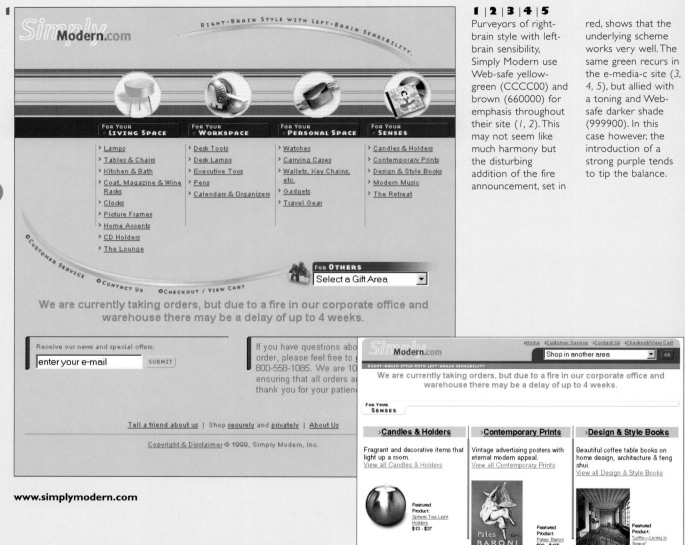

1 | 2 | 3 | 4 | 5

Purveyors of right-brain style with left-brain sensibility, Simply Modern use Web-safe yellow-green (CCCC00) and brown (660000) for emphasis throughout their site (*1, 2*). This may not seem like much harmony but the disturbing addition of the fire announcement, set in red, shows that the underlying scheme works very well. The same green recurs in the e-media-c site (*3, 4, 5*), but allied with a toning and Web-safe darker shade (999900). In this case however, the introduction of a strong purple tends to tip the balance.

www.simplymodern.com

3

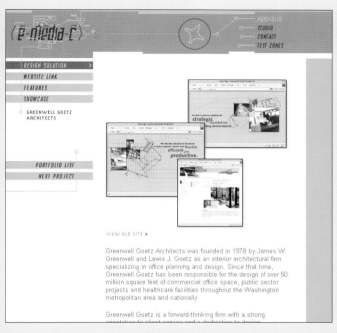

VIEW OLD SITE ▶

Greenwell Goetz Architects was founded in 1978 by James W. Greenwell and Lewis J. Goetz as an interior architectural firm specializing in office planning and design. Since that time, Greenwell Goetz has been responsible for the design of over 50 million square feet of commercial office space, public sector projects and healthcare facilities throughout the Washington metropolitan area and nationally.

Greenwell Goetz is a forward-thinking firm with a strong orientation to client service and a dedication to design

4

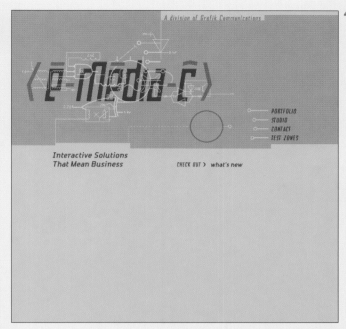

137

www.e-media-c.com

5

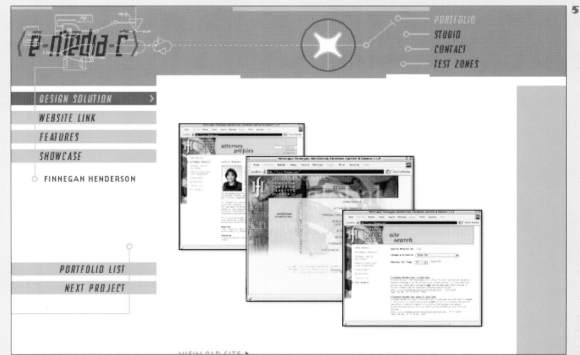

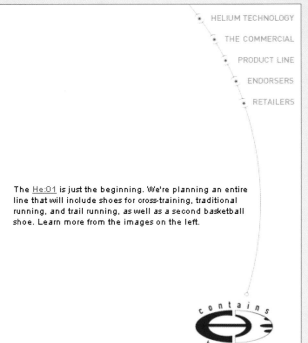

THE

Converse®All Star®

Future

STAY TRUE™

He:01

He:02

CHANY.He

He:01 TRAINING

He:01 RUNNING

HELIUM TECHNOLOGY

THE COMMERCIAL

PRODUCT LINE

ENDORSERS

RETAILERS

The He:01 is just the beginning. We're planning an entire line that will include shoes for cross-training, traditional running, and trail running, as well as a second basketball shoe. Learn more from the images on the left.

contains helium

CONVERSE NEWS

CONTACT CONVERSE

1 | 2 | 3
They're putting helium in your shoes now! The sports shoes manufacturers were very early on the Web, and Converse (1) show that the logo is all, reserving the only contrasting colour for its exclusive use in a sea of white. Solid German investment bankers, Templeton (2, 3), are white as the driven snow as well, with their portfolio manager rendered in a trustworthy blue duotone.

www.converse.com

www.templeton.de

Equal amounts of white, but with discreet doses of hot colour for emphasis, characterize the markedly similar sites of e-business firms, Sapient of the US (4, 5, 6) and PKS in Vienna (7, 8), though the latter allow themselves a zany and mysterious introductory artwork.

139

www.sapient.com

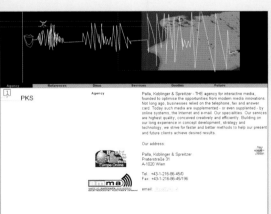

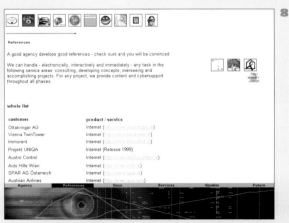

www.pks.at

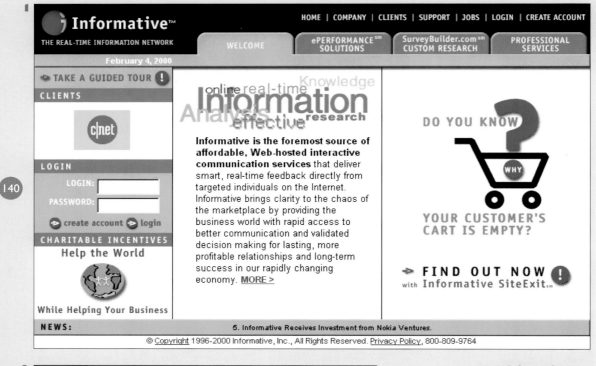

1 | 2 | 3

Once upon a time, there was a visionary, possibly a printer, who invented the tabbed index card. One day his descendants will arrive in town to demand their long overdue royalty payments for the countless billions of occasions upon which the motif has been used on screen. When they come, you'll recognize them easily from their radiused corners and fetching highlights. Still, the tab works, and these two sites confirm that it is a powerful device, especially when allied with strong and contrasting colour.

www.informative.com

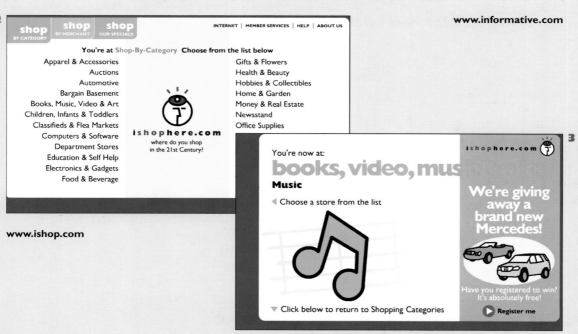

www.ishop.com

4

www.ki-inc.com

5

141

7

6

4 | 5 | 6 | 7
KI Furniture (4, 5, 6)
are tabless and bold
on their homepage,
but they know
curved corners too!
And the shadows that
go with them. Back in
the mainstream, the
trainers' virtual
community site ASTD
(7) struggles in the
frame's straitjacket.

www.astd.org

www.blackbean.com

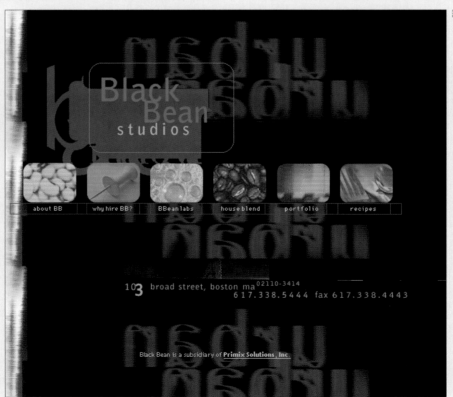

142

143

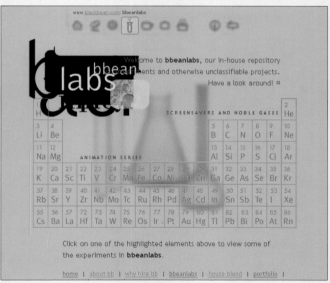

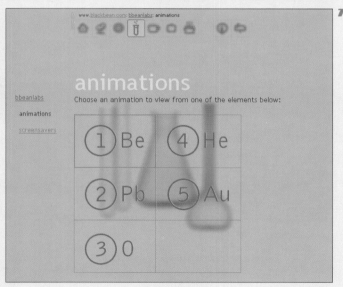

1 | 2 | 3 | 4 | 5 | 6 | 7

Getting the 'poop' on Boston's Black Bean studio is a chromatic sensation worth experiencing. The hoary old Trebuchet MS typeface is given a comprehensive workout in the background, but survives in stinging colour as the screens unfold.

1 |2 |3 |4 |5 |6
Mirco Pasqualini is the enthusiastic creator of Ootworld, (1, 2, 3) an ambitious outpost of Flash-based typographic and colour fun. Equally otherworldly, Heavy.com (4, 5, 6) offer ambitious music tracks served over a bed of Japanese comic art. Both sites can crash your browser.

www.ootworld.com

4

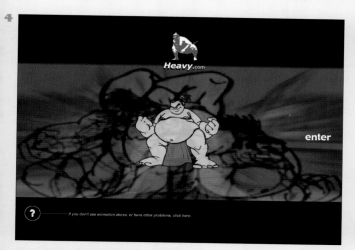

enter

? ─────── if you don't see animation above, or have other problems, click here.

5

SETTINGS | HELP | GET ON THE LIST | CONTACT

LARRY & JACK
PREVIEW

LARRY & JACK
A delightful, whimsical, and
ultimately moronic tale of two
modern-day heroes sworn to
uphold all that is decent in the
timeless milieu of Middle America.

PREVIEW

YOU SUCK | Madison | | | | | | A.K.A. | J.Life | Heavy.com

6

SETTINGS | HELP | GET ON THE LIST | CONTACT

BEHIND THE MUSIC THAT SUCKS
episode#3
Puff Daddy

YOU SUCK | | Madison | BEHIND THE MUSIC | | | | A.K.A. | J.Life | Heavy.com

www.heavy.com

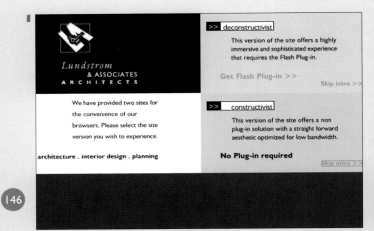

146

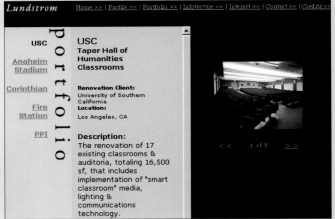

www.lundstrom.com

Two sites which suggest the beginnings of a tradition and its simultaneous destruction. Architects on the Web have adopted the colours of stone, earth, sand and grass as their stock-in-trade (*1, 2, 3, 4*). And they like to build with type. So it is a welcome surprise to find the Ford Mustang heritage site successfully stealing the architects' clothes (*5, 6, 7, 8, 9*).

5

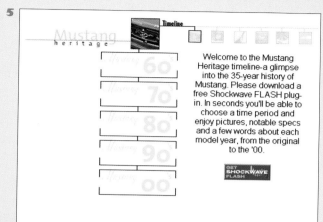

Welcome to the Mustang Heritage timeline-a glimpse into the 35-year history of Mustang. Please download a free Shockwave FLASH plug-in. In seconds you'll be able to choose a time period and enjoy pictures, notable specs and a few words about each model year, from the original to the '00.

6

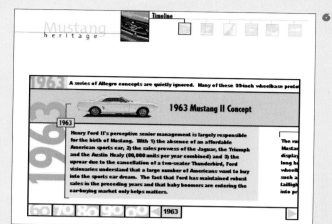

147

7

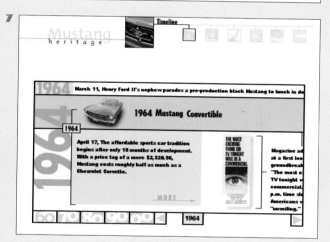

8

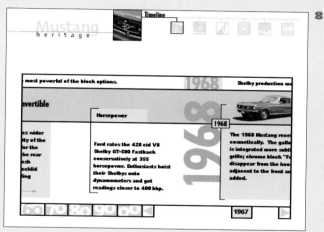

www.fordheritage.com

9

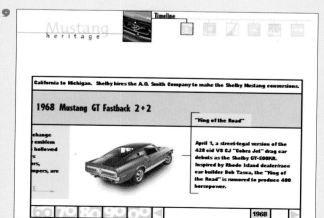

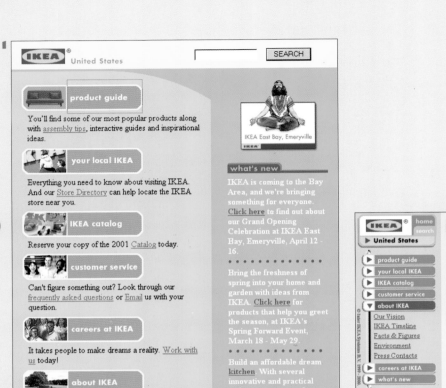

www.ikea-usa.com

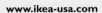

1 | 2 | 3 | 4 | 5 | 6 | 7

Yellow is optimistic and sunny (qualities absolutely essential in the prospective constructor of flat-pack furniture). IKEA runs the entire colour gamut, from the expected cool home page through to an incendiary red 'living with children' screen equipped with green text links. Relax with the IVAR do-it-yourself cupboard building option before attempting the real thing.

4

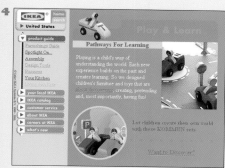

Pathways For Learning

Playing is a child's way of understanding the world. Each new experience builds on the past and creates learning. So we designed children's furniture and toys that are about discovering, creating, pretending and, most importantly, having fun!

Let children create their own world with these KOMMUN sets

Want to Discover?

6

Living With Young Children

Living with children means being prepared for their different stages. One year they might want to be an astronaut, the next a veterinarian. And they need furnishings that adapt easily to their different changes. Luckily, our affordable line of children's products are ready for your child's wild imagination... and their wild adventures!

MAMMUT wardrobe holds clothes, toys and everything else they'll need for their first trip to the moon.

Need More Space?

◄ index ►

5

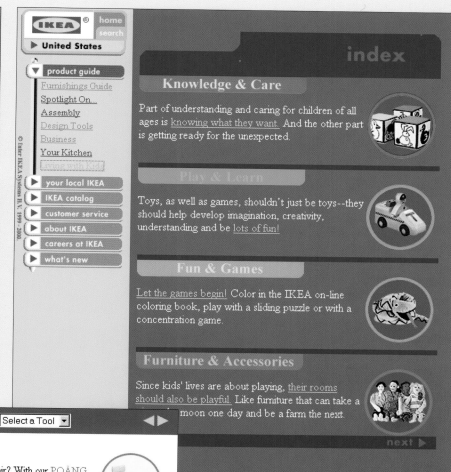

index

Knowledge & Care

Part of understanding and caring for children of all ages is knowing what they want. And the other part is getting ready for the unexpected.

Play & Learn

Toys, as well as games, shouldn't just be toys--they should help develop imagination, creativity, understanding and be lots of fun!

Fun & Games

Let the games begin! Color in the IKEA on-line coloring book, play with a sliding puzzle or with a concentration game.

Furniture & Accessories

Since kids' lives are about playing, their rooms should also be playful. Like furniture that can take a _____ moon one day and be a farm the next.

next ►

149

7

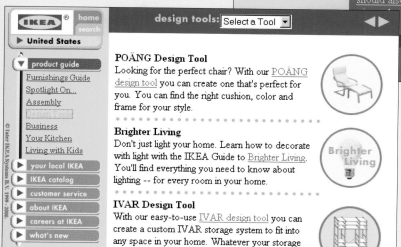

design tools: [Select a Tool ▼] ◄ ►

POÄNG Design Tool

Looking for the perfect chair? With our POÄNG design tool you can create one that's perfect for you. You can find the right cushion, color and frame for your style.

Brighter Living

Don't just light your home. Learn how to decorate with light with the IKEA Guide to Brighter Living. You'll find everything you need to know about lighting -- for every room in your home.

IVAR Design Tool

With our easy-to-use IVAR design tool you can create a custom IVAR storage system to fit into any space in your home. Whatever your storage needs may be, it will help you make the most out of your living area.

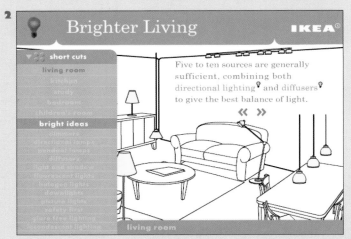

150

www.ikea-usa.com

1 | 2 | 3 | 4 | 5 | 6 | 7 | 8 | 9 | 10

The IKEA site grows organically, with differing design styles to address distinct topics. This is in direct contrast to their printed catalogue output, where uniformity of approach is the rule. The lighting section, for example (1, 2, 3, 4), here takes off on a new colour scheme and monochrome drawing style. So far so good with those shelves...

5

This easy-to-use design tool allows you to create a custom IVAR storage system that will fit into any space. It's perfect for people who need to make the most out of their living area. And the new IVAR components not only fit together, but they also work well with older components, so you can easily update your current system. After you're done creating (or updating) your storage system, you can print out your creation, with a list of IVAR components, to take to your IKEA store.

flexible / room settings / IVAR design tool   IVAR

6

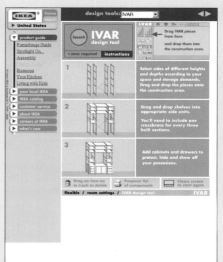

151

7

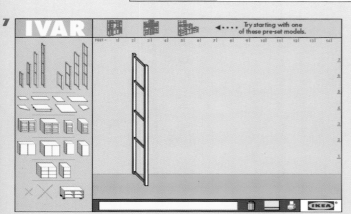

8

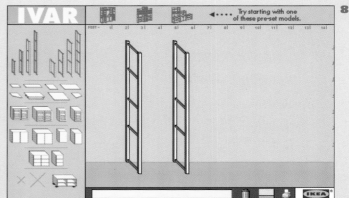

9

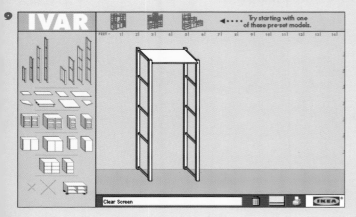

10

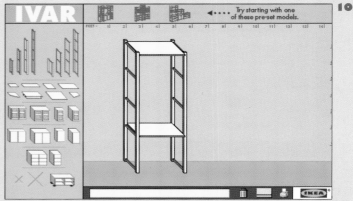

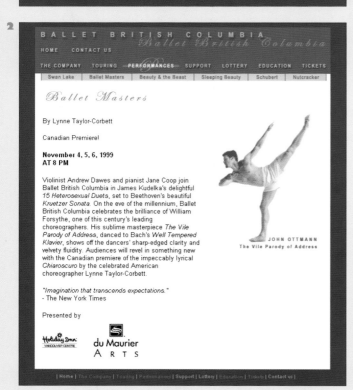

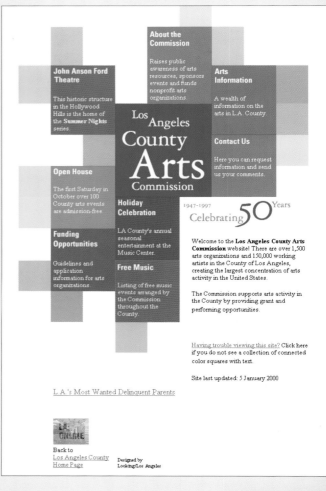

www.balletbc.com

www.lacountyarts.org

1 | 2
Rich chocolate-box
colours with a light
touch of gilt dignify
the Ballet British
Columbia site. Cream
centres for the text
panels and a nicely
judged cream
duotone complete
the picture.

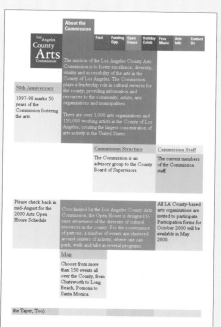

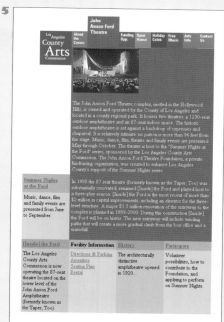

153

3 | 4 | 5 | 6 | 7 | 8
In Los Angeles, the gridlock extends to the city's cultural life. Once accustomed to the layout, however, you'll find the blocks begin to make sense, and the harmonizing colours are a useful unifying device. Charles de Gaulle famously complained that France would never be unified except by fear since it had 265 different kinds of cheese; Los Angeles County has 15,000 working artists.

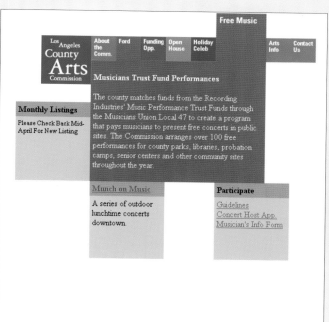

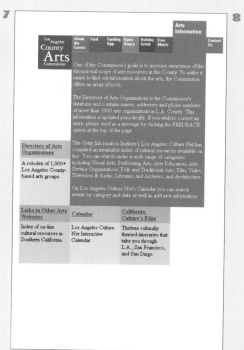

www.ideo.com

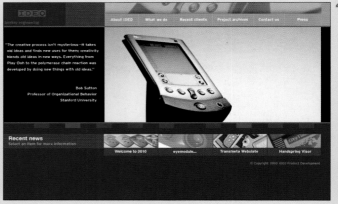

1 | 2 | 3 | 4 | 5 | 6 | 7 | 8 | 9

Industrial designers Ideo take an unconventional line to display their wares. Trusting in the viewer's enthusiasm for horizontal scrolling, the opening blueprint screen offers a grand total of 70 different project studies. The blue ground device continues into each project screen, including that for the new Transmeta Webslate (*1*) which will ultimately sound the death-knell for panoramic presentations like these.

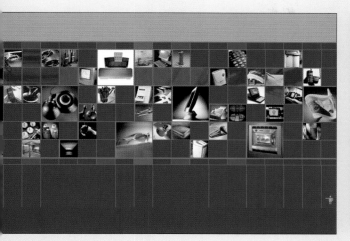

Transmeta | Webslate Concept

IDEO's conceptual design for a modular computer showcases the abilities of the new Crusoe microprocessor from Transmeta. Transmeta commissioned IDEO to design a portable, modular "webslate" concept to demonstrate potential products enabled by their new software-based chip technology. The webslate incorporates a high-resolution, eight-inch touchscreen for viewing web pages, DVD movies, and more. The webslate offers greater portability and more discreet use than a laptop, and offers a larger, more robust viewing area compared to today's handheld PDAs.

IDEO's concept has at its center a slim, two-layer slate which accommodates plug-in modules for various applications. The modules can be added to any of the four sides for landscape or portrait format, and include a camera for on-the-road videoconferencing, a GPS module for navigation, audio speakers and controls for downloaded music, and modules for game playing across the web. A snap-on cover protects the screen and provides a folding

Amtrak | Acela

Amtrak engaged IDEO to propose a strategy for its new high-speed rail service between Boston and Washington, D.C. The challenge was to differentiate rail travel from airlines and automobiles in quality of service across all aspects of the experience of rail travel. IDEO identified ten steps in the passenger's journey, from learning about Amtrak and planning a trip through to arriving at the destination and continuing on.

To understand Amtrak's vision, IDEO's team rode trains, toured stations, interviewed senior management, and analyzed Amtrak's information distribution and advertising campaigns. They conducted in-depth user profiles and studied Amtrak's customer research. This information guided the development of trainset layout and design, a set of station concepts

BBC | Digital Radios

IDEO designed these radio concepts to exploit the advantages of the BBC's new digital broadcast services. IDEO brainstorming generated design ideas which were built into user scenarios to explore the appearance and operation of the radios. Displays on the radios show pictorial information to complement the audio program, such as musician portraits, sports factoids, program guides or recording set-up information. Designs range from home radios that can be instantly personalized by family members to personal portable radios and radios for the shower.

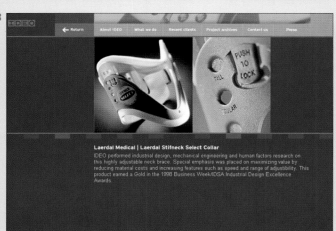

Laerdal Medical | Laerdal Stifneck Select Collar

IDEO performed industrial design, mechanical engineering and human factors research on this highly adjustable neck brace. Special emphasis was placed on maximizing value by reducing material costs and increasing features such as speed and range of adjustability. This product earned a Gold in the 1998 Business Week/IDSA Industrial Design Excellence Awards.

Nike | RV12 Sunglasses

IDEO developed this family of all-terrain eyewear for Nike to address particular issues encountered while traveling on diverse surfaces. New wraparound lenses increased downward and peripheral fields of view and the "flying lens" design improves airflow and decreases fogging. The glasses employ a flexible sub-frame to better fit a variety of head sizes and a rubberized nosepiece and (on the RV12) rubberized temples provide better stability and comfort. In addition, the optics have been de-centered to provide accurate depth perception on shifting trail surfaces.

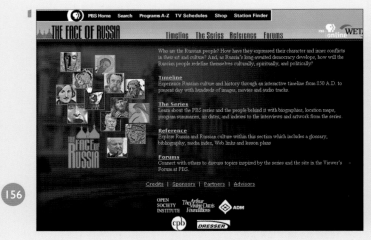

156

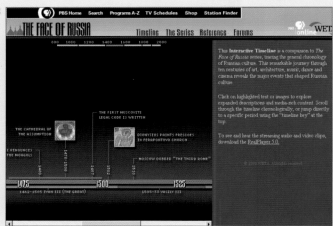

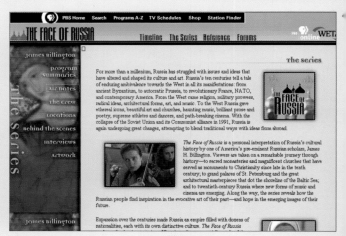

www.pbs.org

1 | 2 | 3 | 4

The 'Face of Russia' site uses opulent reds and golds to suggest both Russia's imperial history and its more recent communist past. Extensive vertical and horizontal colour graduations offer the site hostage to low-grade browsers, but the strong overall colour design keeps it all together.

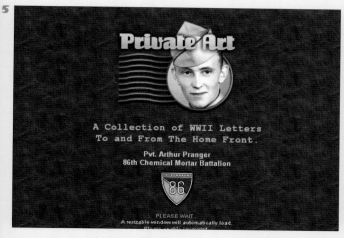

157

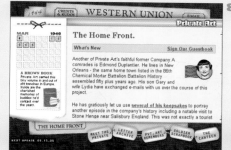

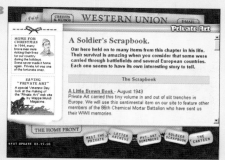

5 | 6 | 7 | 8 | 9 | 10

The Private Art(hur Pranger) site is a careful tribute to a lost world, dressed in the colours of faded fatigues. It is curious that our perception of this era makes this site look authentic; the small amount of 'natural colour' film shot at the time, though rarely known, is shocking in its bright intensity.

www.private-art.com

158

1

2

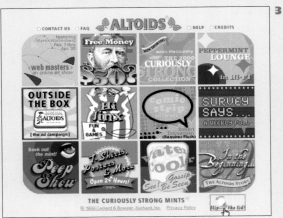

3

www.altoids.com

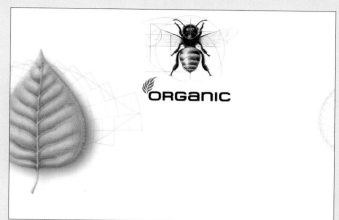

159

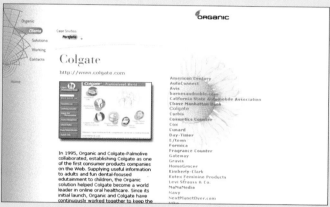

1 | 2 | 3 | 4 | 5 | 6 | 7 | 8

These two sites, though their fields of operation could hardly be more different, show the Web at what it does best – illusion and association. Altoids mints are 12mm (half an inch) in diameter and taste strongly of peppermint, but not more strongly, to this observer, than similar confectionery. This whimsical site (1, 2, 3), however, manages to invest them with a range of typographic associations which employ devices from every corner of the Web portfolio, all wrapped in a pale fondant background. At first sight, Organic (4, 5, 6, 7, 8) might appear to be selling health food – there are bees and leaves aplenty – but no, it's e-business in another coat. Leonardo's man in a circle would spin in his grave if he knew that the leaves had been designed in FreeHand.

www.organic.com

A rosy glow pervades the Delphi Ventures site. Old pre-press operators would have toiled for hours to lose the magenta cast in the headline transparencies, but we are now so familiar with deliberately shifting colour balance that they slide by almost unnoticed. Deep blue, it should be noted, is the colour of financial probity, and may be renamed Banker's Blue in some future Web specification.

www.delphiventures.com

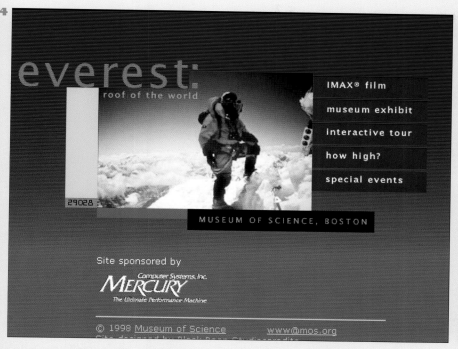

6

8

4 | 5 | 6 | 7 | 8
With the aid of IMAX cinema, you can now virtually stand on the summit of Everest. Boston Museum of Science's Everest site elegantly sets off the hard-won images on rich grounds of saturated colour.

www.mos.org

1 | 2 | 3
Juxt Interactive uses Flash to create a highly mannered movie which borrows heavily from the old typography. This simple approach contrasts with the fearsome bazaar of their home page (*1*).

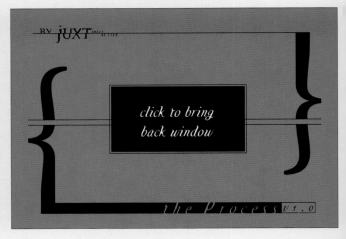

www.juxtinteractive.com

welcome | choose your version   **flash   html   palm**

www.nexus-group.de

5

4 | 5 | 6
Flash is to the fore also at Nexus, but in conjunction with a cool European look. Twinkling monochrome panels chase each other round the headline bar, vestiges of hairline rules distinguish the restrained type design.

164

1 | 2
Nike now offer home movies to those who are disinclined to jog to the cinema. And there are other advantages – you can view the action in any order you choose. The tabbed navigation bars carry posterized GIFs, the bars themselves cast shadows on the background.

www.nike.com

travel.disney.go.com

3 | 4 | 5

165

Virtuoso frame
design from Disney.
All is light, bright and
enthusiastic. Toy Story
rates a checkerplate
background, but
otherwise, the
colour values and
backgrounds are
utterly familiar.

www.disney.co.uk

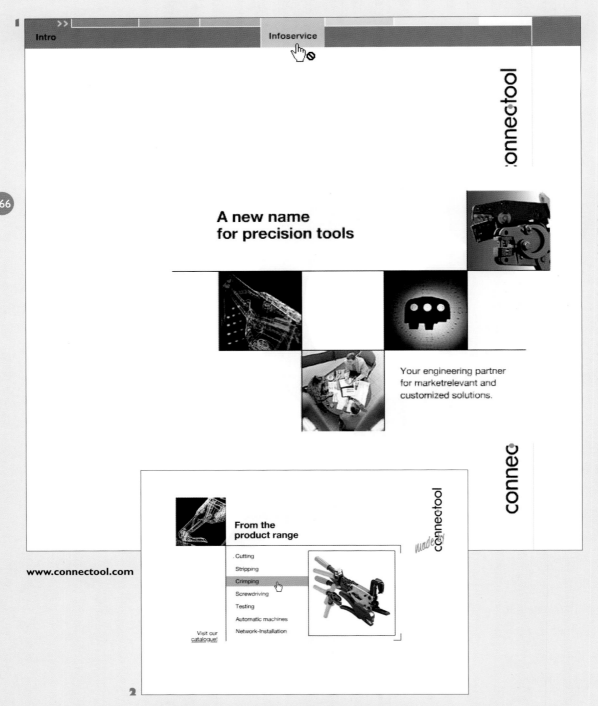

1 | **2** | **3** | **4** | **5** | **6**
Cutting, stripping and
crimping; not
hairdressing but high
quality metal-bashing.
The Connectool site
(*1, 2*) is an object
lesson in how to
dignify the prosaic
industrial object in
an elegant design
environment. Spot
colour is only used in
the corporate logo,
while tiny pictures of
the product float
across a large white
ground. In the world
of racing, Acer adopt
a similar approach (*3,
4, 5*) but with an even
more sparing use of
colour. It takes only
one inadvertent finger
movement to land up
in the less discreet
reaches of page
design (*6*).

166

3

Products About Contact Store

ACER**RACING**

IT'S ABOUT THE RACE
TAKE IT TO THE NEXT LEVEL

[Select your product]

Competition accessories **precision** tested in the labs
and proven on the track. You can feel the difference
with ACER Racing. Take it to the next level.

This site realized by **EN**VISION
interactive

4

Products About Contact Store | Home

ACER**RACING**

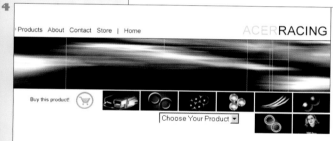

Buy this product!

Choose Your Product

Statistics and information

**ULTRA O PERFORMANCE SERIES
SUSPENSION O RINGS**

The only professional suspension o-ring to
combine the lowest coefficient of friction, internal
lubrication, and the highest tear resistance. The
longest lasting, smoothest o-ring **ever** for the
smoothest suspension movement. What can
these o-rings do for you?

▸ **Extend rebuild intervals**

www.acerracing.com

6

www.aceracing.com

5

Products About Contact Store | Home

ACER**RACING**

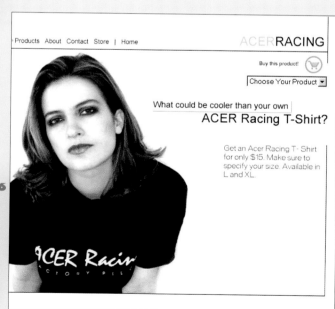

Buy this product!

Choose Your Product

What could be cooler than your own
ACER Racing T-Shirt?

Get an Acer Racing T- Shirt
for only $15. Make sure to
specify your size. Available in
L and XL.

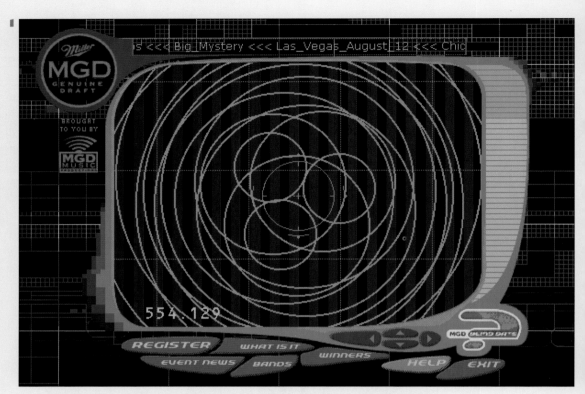

 1 | 2
Cultural confusion in Milwaukee. Beer is now music. And the light blond hues of the product are nowhere to be seen. Java and Flash drive a frantic dark palette of opposing red and blue against the customary techno graph paper.

168

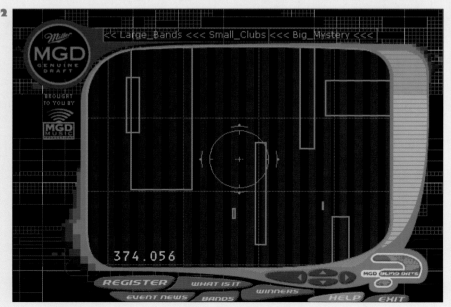

www.mgdtaproom.com

3

www.binding.de

www.grolsch.nl

5

6

4

www.fullers.co.uk

3 | 4 | 5 | 6
Four European
breweries tackle the
art of promotion in
more conventional
style.

www.chimay.com

1 | 2
Welcome, in German and Italian. Druckindustrie Nord printers (1) plant an elegant foot in the digital doorway. Gone is the usual printer's identity of oversize CMYK dots and fluttering sheets of paper – there remains only a faint shadow of meshing cogs in the background. Giglio (2) adopts the same grey and orange uniform for its Sicilian fashion store.

www.vdnord.de

www.giglio.com

www.fujifilm.com

www.josecuervo.com

3

4

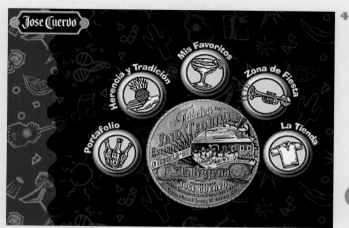

171

5

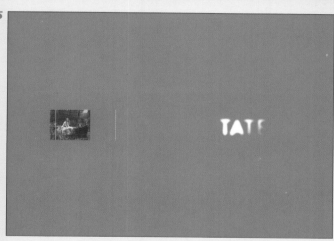

6

1 | 2 | 3 | 4

Web-page design is merely a branch of cooking; whatever the ingredients, the plate must appear appetizing. These four examples of the chromatic present are pointers to the immediate future. Fuji offers cool interactive cartography over a salad bed of their house packaging colour. The UK's Tate Modern galler, opens up with a soft jelly logo drizzled over raspberry sauce. Cuervo tequila clings joyfully to heritage design on a bed of modern Mexicana. And the flatulent buffet from hell. Time for a lie down.

www.tate.org.uk

www.goa.org.uk

HTML COLOUR MECHANICS

The tiny rosette of dots that is the basis of the four-colour print process makes a dull bouquet alongside the monitor's glowing phosphors. Although the printed page has a fundamental resolution about four times finer than the screen, its apparent superiority is more than negated by the screen's much greater contrast range and highly saturated colour values. The typical user, moreover, sits at least twice as far away from the screen as from a book, adding more apparent sharpness to the screen image.

With sufficient processing power, current monitors can deliver over 16 million different colours. This is as near 'true' colour as makes no practical difference. Prehistoric monitors could only turn pixels on and off – screens were black-and-white (or, variously, black and green or orange). This was 'one-bit' colour depth, and great was the joy in the land when the frontiers were gradually pushed back through four-bit, giving 16 (2^4) colours, and then the eight-bit 256 (2^8) games standard, right up to 24-bit (2^{24}) with 16,777,216 colours.

Large numbers of this order won't work reliably on the Web. A handy compromise for now is a 256-colour range. Subtract the 40 colours demanded for its own purposes by the computer's operating system, and you are left with 216. This offers an elegant cube with six units per edge. Another sum: 6 x 6 x 6 = 216. A cube has eight convenient corners – and the red, green and blue electron guns at the back of the screen, when either full on or off, can produce eight combinations of colour.

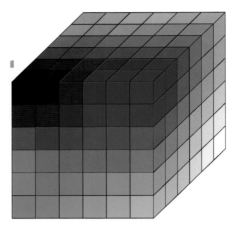

1
The 216-colour cube shows seven of its eight corners (*left*). Yellow (red and green mixed at full strength) is hidden at the back left corner.

Put these extremes at the corners of the cube and string the intermediate colours along each edge to give a 20% difference between each colour. In other words, the guns have a six-step range between 0 (completely off) and 255 (full on).

2
Filleted out, the cube reveals all 216 colours (*right*). Black (no signal at all) and white (all three guns full on) are found at diagonally opposite corners.

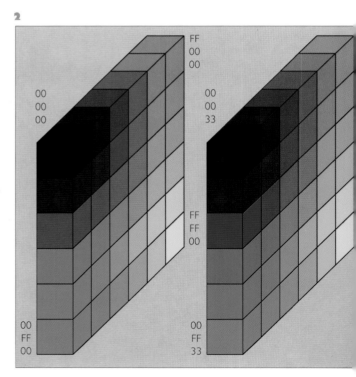

FF
00
00

00
00
00

00
00
33

FF
FF
00

00
FF
00

00
FF
33

Only one hurdle remains. The computer needs a single character to represent numeric values. Hexadecimal comes to the rescue. In hexadecimal there are 16 values, represented by the numerals 0–9 followed by the characters A–F. Only six of these values concern us here, because of the 20% gap between one value and the next. In HTML code, colours are represented by settings for the red/green/blue guns in the paired form rrggbb. Since it's difficult to visualize a colour labelled CC0033, Web-design software conceals the mathematics and calls it 'pinkish red'. Such programs will accept intermediate colours (like B0C4DE 'light steel blue'), but they will appear dithered on 256-colour screens.

The flattened cube is shown (within the limitations of the four-colour process) on the following two pages. The two subsequent pages then show patches of 18 selected colours overlaid with 12 different shades.

3

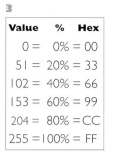

Value	%	Hex
0 =	0% =	00
51 =	20% =	33
102 =	40% =	66
153 =	60% =	99
204 =	80% =	CC
255 =	100% =	FF

4

R	G	B	
00	00	00	= ■
00	00	FF	= ■
FF	00	FF	= ■
FF	00	00	= ■
00	FF	00	= ■
00	FF	FF	= ■
FF	FF	00	= ■
FF	FF	FF	= □
33	33	33	= ■
66	66	66	= ■
99	99	99	= ■
CC	CC	CC	= ■

3 | 4
Numeric, percentage and hexadecimal compared (above). Only these values are 'Web-safe' on 256-colour screens. Hexadecimal settings of the three guns (right) show the cube's corner values, followed by the only four available greys.

175

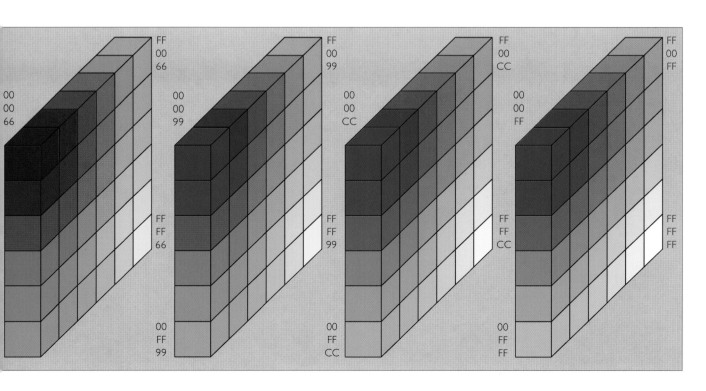

330000	333300	336600	339900	33CC00	33FF00	66FF00	66CC00	669900
330033	333333	336633	339933	33CC33	33FF33	66FF33	66CC33	669933
330066	333366	336666	339966	33CC66	33FF66	66FF66	66CC66	669966
330099	333399	336699	339999	33CC99	33FF99	66FF99	66CC99	669999
3300CC	3333CC	3366CC	3399CC	33CCCC	33FFCC	66FFCC	66CCCC	6699CC
3300FF	3333FF	3366FF	3399FF	33CCFF	33FFFF	66FFFF	66CCFF	6699FF
0000FF	0033FF	0066FF	0099FF	00CCFF	00FFFF	99FFFF	99CCFF	9999FF
0000CC	0033CC	0066CC	0099CC	00CCCC	00FFCC	99FFCC	99CCCC	9999CC
000099	003399	006699	009999	00CC99	00FF99	99FF99	99CC99	999999
000066	003366	006666	009966	00CC66	00FF66	99FF66	99CC66	999966
000033	003333	006633	009933	00CC33	00FF33	99FF33	99CC33	999933
000000	003300	006600	009900	00CC00	00FF00	99FF00	99CC00	999900

666600	663300	660000	FF0000	FF3300	FF6600	FF9900	FFCC00	FFFF00
666633	663333	660033	FF0033	FF3333	FF6633	FF9933	FFCC33	FFFF33
666666	663366	660066	FF0066	FF3366	FF6666	FF9966	FFCC66	FFFF66
666699	663399	660099	FF0099	FF3399	FF6699	FF9999	FFCC99	FFFF99
6666CC	6633CC	6600CC	FF00CC	FF33CC	FF66CC	FF99CC	FFCCCC	FFFFCC
6666FF	6633FF	6600FF	FF00FF	FF33FF	FF66FF	FF99FF	FFCCFF	FFFFFF
9966FF	9933FF	9900FF	CC00FF	CC33FF	CC66FF	CC99FF	CCCCFF	CCFFFF
9966CC	9933CC	9900CC	CC00CC	CC33CC	CC66CC	CC99CC	CCCCCC	CCFFCC
996699	993399	990099	CC0099	CC3399	CC6699	CC9999	CCCC99	CCFF99
996666	993366	990066	CC0066	CC3366	CC6666	CC9966	CCCC66	CCFF66
996633	993333	990033	CC0033	CC3333	CC6633	CC9933	CCCC33	CCFF33
996600	993300	990000	CC0000	CC3300	CC6600	CC9900	CCCC00	CCFF00

177

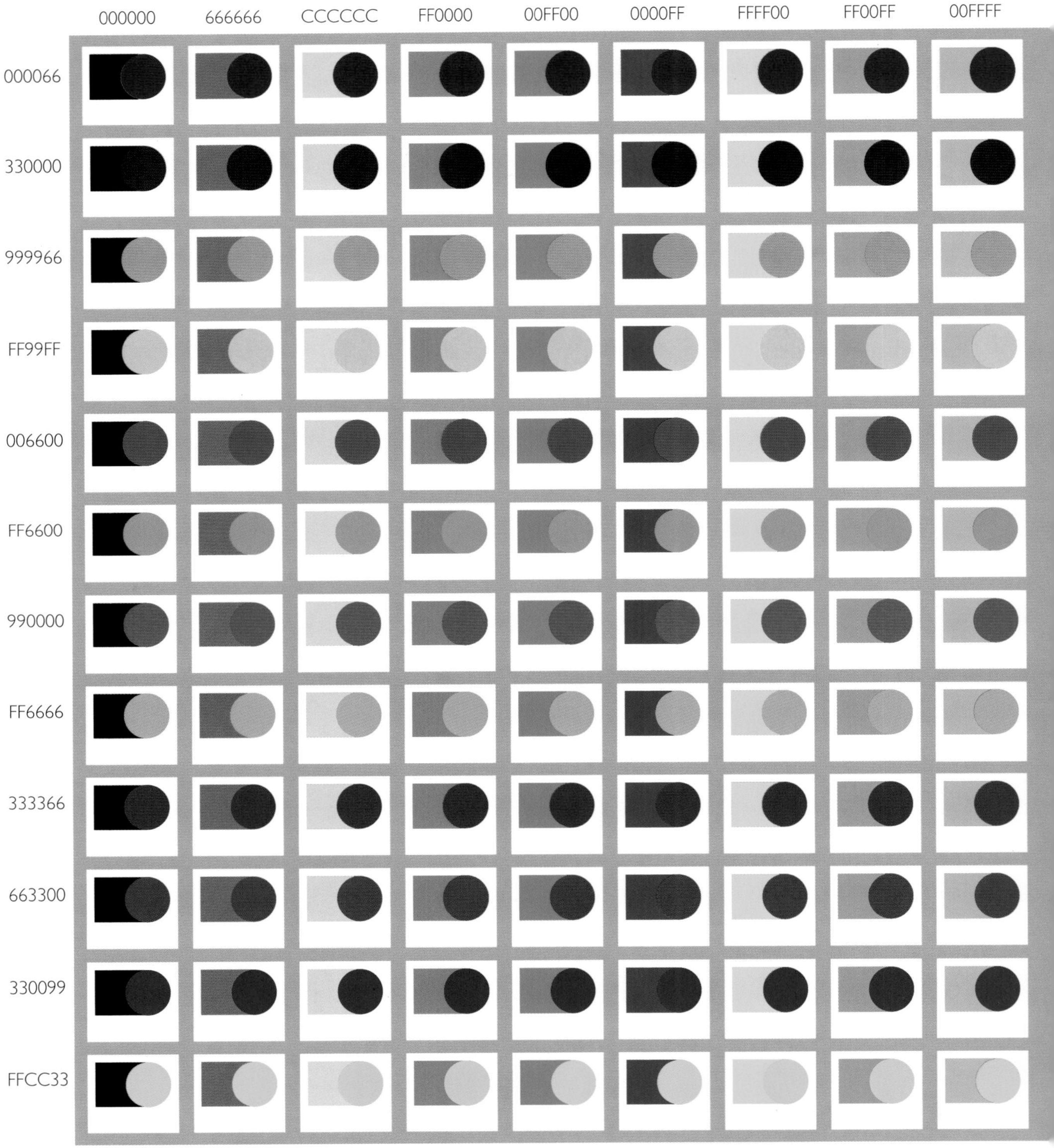
000000
666666
CCCCCC
FF0000
00FF00
0000FF
FFFF00
FF00FF
00FFFF
000066
330000
999966
FF99FF
006600
FF6600
990000
FF6666
333366
663300
330099
FFCC33

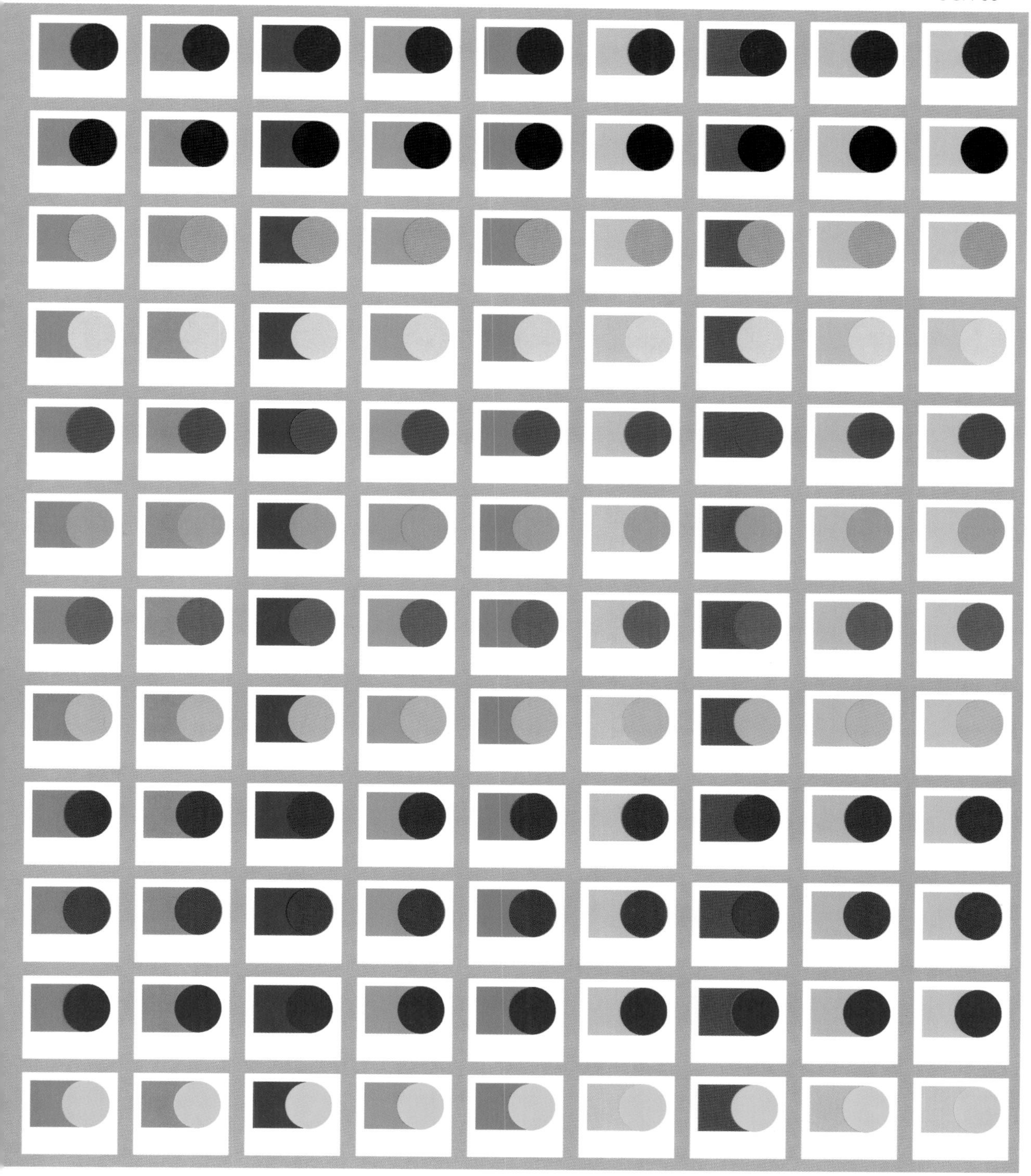

CC0000	CC00CC	0000CC	00CCCC	00CC00	CCCC00	336633	99CC99	CCFF66	

000066

330000

999966

FF99FF

179

006600

FF6600

990000

FF6666

333366

663300

330099

FFCC33

GLOSSARY

4-bit The allocation of four bits of memory to each pixel, giving an image or screen display of 16 greys or colours (a row of four bits can be written in 16 different combinations: 0000, 0001, 1001, 0110, etc).

8-bit Of display monitors or digital images – the allocation of eight data bits to each pixel, producing a display or image of 256 greys or colours (a row of eight bits can be written in 256 different combinations: 0000000, 00000001, 10000001, 00111100, and so on).

16-bit colour A facility in some image-editing applications, such as Photoshop, that allows you to work on images in 16-bit-per-channel mode rather than 8-bit mode – RGB images use three 8-bit channels (totalling 24 bits), whereas CMYK images use four 8-bit channels (totalling 32 bits). A 16-bit-per-channel image provides finer control over colour but, because an RGB image totals 48 bits (16 × 3) and a CMYK image totals 64 bits (16 × 4), the resulting file size is considerably larger than an 8-bit-per-channel image.

24-bit colour The allocation of 24 bits of memory to each pixel, giving a possible screen display of 16.7 million colours (a row of 24 bits can be written in 16.7 million different combinations of 0s and 1s). Twenty-four bits are required for CMYK separations – eight bits for each.

absolute colorimetry Calibrating the colour performance of a device relative to an 'absolute' CIE white (e.g. D50), rather than to the device's natural white point.

achromatic A colour that has no saturation, or 'chroma', such as black or white.

additive colours The colour model describing the primary colours of transmitted light: red, green and blue (RGB). Additive colours can be mixed to form all other colours in photographic reproduction and computer display monitors.

adjustment profile An adjustment that alters image appearance, applied during the creation of a link.

alpha channel A place where information regarding the transparency of a pixel is kept. In image files this is a separate channel – additional to the three RGB or four CMYK channels – where 'masks' are stored, simulating the physical material used in platemaking to shield parts of the plate from light.

anti-aliasing A technique of optically eliminating the jagged effect of bitmapped images or text reproduced on low-resolution devices such as monitors. This is achieved by blending the colour at the edges of the object with its background by averaging the density of the range of pixels involved. Anti-aliasing is also sometimes employed to filter texture maps, such as those used in 3-D applications, to prevent moiré patterns.

ASCII *(pronounced 'asskee')* Acronym for the American Standard Code for Information Interchange, a code that assigns a number to the 256 letters, numbers and symbols (including carriage returns and tabs) that can be typed on a keyboard. ASCII is the cross-platform, computer industry-standard, text-only file format.

attribute (1) The specification applied to a character, box or other item. Character attributes include font, size, style, colour, shade, scaling, kerning etc.

attribute (2) A characteristic of an HTML tag that is identified alongside the tag in order to describe it.

background The area of an image upon which the principal subject, or foreground, sits.

background colour/tint In graphics applications, a colour or tint that has been applied to the background of any item, such as a page, text box or illustration.

banding An aberration that occurs in the electronic reproduction of graduated tints, when the ratio of halftone screen ruling and output resolution is incorrect, causing a 'stepped' appearance. The maximum number of achievable levels of tone is 256 (the PostScript limit) for each of the four process colours (CMYK); so to calculate the optimum imagesetter resolution, multiply the halftone screen ruling by 16 (the square root of 256 – each imagesetter dot is constructed on a matrix of 16 × 16 pixels). Therefore, to minimize the chance of banding in a single colour image to be printed with a halftone screen ruling of 150lpi, the maximum levels of grey can be achieved if it is output by the imagesetter at 2400dpi (150 × 16). Banding can also occur when the percentage values of a large area of a graduated single colour tint are very close (40–50%, for example).

binary system An arithmetical system that uses 2 as its base, meaning that it can only be represented by two possible values – 1 or 0, on or off, something or nothing, negative or positive, small or large, etc.

binary code The computer code, based on 1 or 0, that is used to represent a character or instruction. For example, the binary code 01100010 represents a lower case 'b'.

binary file A file in which data is described in binary code rather than text. Binary files typically hold pictures, sounds or a complete application program.

bit A commonly used acronym for binary digit, the smallest piece of information a computer can use. Each alphabet character requires eight bits (called a **byte**) to store it.

bit density The number of bits occupying a particular area or length – per inch of magnetic tape, for example.

bit depth The number of bits assigned to each pixel on a monitor, scanner or image file. One-bit, for example, will only produce black and white (the bit is either on or off), whereas 8-bit will generate 256 greys or colours (256 is the maximum number of permutations of a string of eight 1s and 0s), and 24-bit will produce 16.7 million colours (256 × 256 × 256). Also called **colour depth**.

bitmap Strictly speaking, any text character or image composed of dots. A bitmap is a 'map' describing the location and binary state (on or off) of 'bits'; it defines the complete collection of pixels or dots that comprise an image (on a monitor, for example).

bitmapped font A font in which the characters are made up of dots, or pixels, as distinct from an outline font, which is drawn from vectors. Bitmapped fonts generally accompany PostScript 'Type 1' fonts and are used to render the fonts' shape on screen (they are sometimes called screen fonts). To draw the shape accurately on screen, your computer must have a bitmap installed for each size

GLOSSARY

181

(they are also called fixed-size fonts), although this is not necessary if you have ATM installed, as this uses the outline, or printer version, of the font. TrueType fonts are 'outline' and so do not require a bitmapped version.

bitmapped graphic An image made up of dots, or pixels, and usually generated by paint or image-editing applications, as distinct from the vector images of object-oriented drawing applications.

black generation The process of creating the black channel, and its effects on the colour channels when converting RGB to CMYK.

blend(ing) The merging of two or more colours, forming a gradual transition from one to the other. Most graphics applications offer the facility for creating blends from any mix and any percentage of process colours. The quality of the blend is limited by the number of shades of a single colour that can be reproduced without visible 'banding'. Since this limit is determined by the PostScript maximum of 256 levels, banding may become more visible when the values of a single colour are very close (30%–60%, for example). However, blending two or more colours reduces the risk of banding.

brightness The amount of light reflected by a colour.

brightness range The range of tones in a photographic subject, from the darkest to the lightest.

bump map A bitmap image file, normally greyscale, most frequently used in 3-D applications for modifying surfaces or applying textures. The grey values in the image are assigned height values, with black representing the troughs and white the peaks. Bump maps are used in the form of digital elevation models (DEMs) for generating cartographic relief maps.

byte A single group made up of eight bits (0s and 1s) that is processed as one unit. It is possible to configure eight 0s and 1s in only 256 different permutations; thus a byte can represent any value between 0 and 255 – the maximum number of ASCII characters, one byte being required for each.

CAD (computer-aided design) Any design carried out using a computer. However, the term is generally used with reference to 3-D design, such as product design or architecture, where a computer software application is used to construct and develop complex structures.

CAD/CAM (computer-aided design and manufacture) Any manufacturing process in which computers are used to assist and control the entire operation from initial concept to finished product.

calibration The process of adjusting a machine or item of hardware to conform to a known scale or standard so that it performs more accurately. In graphic reproduction it is important that the various devices and materials used in the production chain, such as scanners, monitors, imagesetters and printing presses, conform to a consistent set of measures in order to achieve true fidelity, particularly where colour is concerned. Calibration of reproduction and display devices is generally carried out with a **densitometer**.

characterization Measuring the colour characteristics of a device and comparing the measurements to standard reference values. In colour management, the measure of these deviations results in a device profile.

chroma The intensity, or purity, of a colour; thus its degree of saturation.

chromaticity The hue and saturation of a colour sample.

Cibachrome A proprietary process for obtaining photographic colour prints directly from transparencies, developed by Agfa.

CIE (Commission Internationale de l'Eclairage) International organization which defined a visual colour model that forms the basis for colorimetric measurements of colour.

CIE L*a*b* colour space A three-dimensional colour model based on the system devised by CIE for measuring colour. L*a*b* colour is designed to maintain consistent colour regardless of the kind of device used to create or output the image, whether a scanner, monitor or printer. L*a*b* colour consists of a luminance or lightness component (L) and two chromatic components: green to red (a) and blue to yellow (b). Without the asterisks, it is the internal colour model used by Adobe Photoshop when converting from one colour mode to another; and 'Lab mode' is useful for working with Kodak PhotoCD images. CIE L*a*b* values are mathematically convenient but non-intuitive to most people, hence L*a*b* colour editing tools are uncommon.

CIE XYZ A CIE colour space defined in three dimensions (XYZ). These coordinates represent the amount of red, green and blue light necessary to match a specific colour.

CLUT Acronym for Colour Look-Up Table. A preset table of colours (to a maximum of 256) that the operating system uses when in 8-bit mode. CLUTs are also attached to individual images saved in 8-bit 'indexed' mode – that is, when an application converts a 24-bit image (one with millions of colours) to 8-bit, it draws up a table ('index') of up to 256 of the most frequently used colours in the image (the total number of colours depending on where the image will be viewed – Mac, Windows or Web, for example). If a colour in the original image does not appear in the table, the application either chooses the closest one or simulates it by 'dithering' colours that are available in the table.

CMY (cyan, magenta, yellow) The primary colours of the 'subtractive' colour model, created when you subtract red, green or blue from white light. In other words, if an object reflects green and blue light but absorbs (subtracts) red, then it will appear to you as cyan. Cyan, magenta and yellow are the basic printing-process colours.

CMYK (cyan, magenta, yellow and black) The four printing-process colours based on the subtractive colour model (black is represented by the letter K, which stands for key plate). In colour reproduction most of the colours are achieved by cyan, magenta and yellow, the theory being that when all three are combined they produce black. However, this is rarely achievable – and would be undesirable since too much ink would be used, causing problems with drying time etc. For this reason, black is used to add density to darker areas – while, to compensate, smaller amounts of the other colours are used (this also has cost benefits, since black is cheaper than coloured inks). The degree of colour that is 'removed' is calculated by a technique known as undercolour removal (UCR).

Color-Key™ A proprietary dry-proofing system developed by 3M.

ColorSync Apple Computer's implementation of the ICC standard.

colour The visual interpretation of the various wavelengths of reflected or refracted light.

colour bar The colour device printed on the edge of colour proofs or in the trim area of press sheets which enables the repro house and printer to check — by eye or with instruments — the fidelity of colour separations and the accuracy of printing. The colour bar helps to monitor such things as ink density, paper stability, dot gain, trapping, and so on. Also called a 'codet'.

colour break The edge between two areas of colour in an image.

colour cast A bias in a colour image that can be either intentional or undesirable. If the former, it is usually made at proof-correction stage to enhance the colour of an image; if the latter, the cast could be due to any of a number of causes occurring when the image was photographed, scanned, manipulated on computer, output, proofed or printed.

colour chart A printed reference chart used in colour reproduction to select or match colour tints made from percentage variations of the four process colours. When using a colour chart, for absolute accuracy you should have one prepared by your chosen printer and printed on the actual paper that will be used for the job — a situation that, in practice, is highly unlikely.

colour correction The process of adjusting colour values in reproduction in order to achieve the desired result. Although this can occur at scanning or image-manipulation stage, colour correction is generally carried out after 'wet' proofing (proofs created using process-colour inks) or, as a very limited last resort, on press.

colour engine A software utility that applies links to images to transform them from one mode to another.

colour filters Thin sheets of transparent material, such as glass or gelatin, placed over a camera lens to modify the quality of light or colours in an image.

colour gamut Gamut, or **colour space**, describes the full range of colours achievable by any single device on the reproduction chain. While the visible spectrum contains many millions of colours, not all of them are achievable by all devices and, even if the colour gamuts for different devices overlap, they will never match exactly — for example, the 16.7 million colours that can be displayed on a monitor cannot be printed on a commercial four-colour press. For this reason, various colour-management systems (CMS) have been devised to maintain consistency of colour gamuts across various devices.

colorimeter A device that is used for measuring tristimulus values (the quantities of RGB, see **tristimulus values**).

colorimetric Measured or expressed in terms of tristimulus values (quantities of RGB).

colour library An application support file that contains predefined colours. These may be the application's default colours, or colours defined by you, or other predefined colour palettes or tables.

colour-management module (CMM) A profile for managing and matching colours accurately across different platforms and devices. CMMs conform to a colour-management system (CMS), such as that defined by the International Colour Consortium (ICC). CMMs interpret the ICC profiles that describe the RGB and CMYK colour spaces on your computer. There are usually ICC profiles installed on your computer by ICC-compliant applications such as Adobe Photoshop; or you can create your own. The selected profile is then embedded in the image you are working on, so that it can later be used as a reference by other devices in the production process. You may find a variety of CMMs already on your computer: those built in to ICC-compliant applications (usually the best if you are unsure of how to use CMMs); the Kodak Digital Science Colour Management System® (primarily for use with images using the Kodak PhotoCD format); or CMMs specified by the computer's operating system, such as Apple ColorSync and Microsoft ICM.

colour-management system (CMS) The name given to a method devised to provide accuracy and consistency of colour representation across all devices in the colour-reproduction chain — scanners, monitors, printers, imagesetters and so on. Typical CMSs include the ones defined by the International Color Consortium (ICC), Kodak's Digital Science Color Management System, Apple's ColorSync and Microsoft's ICM.

colour model The method of defining or modifying colour. Although there are many proprietary colour models, such as PANTONE®, FOCOLTONE, TRUMATCH, TOYO and DIC, the two generic models are those based on the way light is transmitted — the 'additive' and 'subtractive' colour models. The additive colour model is used, for example, in computer monitors, which transmit varying proportions of red, green and blue (RGB) light which we interpret as different colours. By combining the varying intensities of RGB light, we can simulate the range of colours found in nature. When 100 per cent values of all three are combined, we perceive white; and if there is no light, we see nothing or, rather, black. The subtractive colour model is based on the absorption (i.e. subtraction) and reflection of light. Printing inks are an example of this — if you subtract 100 per cent values of either red, green or blue from white light, you create cyan, magenta or yellow.

colour picker (1) A colour model displayed on a computer monitor. Colour pickers may be specific to an application such as Adobe Photoshop, or to a third-party colour model such as PANTONE®, or to the operating system running on your computer.

colour picker (2) A book of printed colour samples that are carefully defined and graded, from which you can select spot colours. Colour pickers generally conform to a colour model, such as PANTONE®, so you can be confident that the colour you choose will be faithfully reproduced by the printer — unlike a 'colour chart', which is generally used to select colours made up from process-colour inks.

colour space See **colour gamut**.

colour swatch A sample of a specific colour, taken either from a colour chart or colour picker, or from some other printed example, and used as a guide either for specification or reproduction of spot colours or process tints.

colour table A predefined table, or 'index', of colours used to determine a specific colour model – for example, for converting an image to CMYK. A colour table, or 'CLUT', also describes the palette of colours used to display an image.

colour temperature A measure, or composition, of light. This is defined as the temperature – measured in degrees Kelvin (a scale based on absolute darkness rising to incandescence) – to which a black object would need to be heated to produce a particular colour of light. A tungsten lamp, for example, measures 2,900°K, whereas the temperature of direct sunlight is around 5,000°K and is considered the ideal viewing standard in the graphic arts.

colour transparency (film) A photographic image on transparent film generated, after processing, as a positive image. Colour transparencies are ideal as originals for colour separations for process printing because they offer a greater range of colours than is provided by reflective prints. Colour-transparency film is supplied for a variety of camera formats – typically 35mm, 2¼in square and 4 × 5in. Colour transparencies are also variously known as trannies, colour trannies, slides (which generally refers to 35mm) and colour-reversal film.

colour value The tonal value of a colour when related to a light-to-dark scale of pure greys.

colour wheel Circular diagram representing the complete spectrum of visible colours.

commercial colour The term (sometimes used derogatorily) applied to colour images generated by desktop scanners, as opposed to high-resolution reproduction scanners.

complementary colours Two colours directly opposite each other on the colour wheel that, when combined, form white or black, depending on the colour model (subtractive or additive).

Component Video A QuickTime 'codec' (compression setting) that generates a 2:1 compression. Being limited to 16-bit colour depth, it is best suited to archiving movies.

composite colour file The low-resolution file that combines the four CMYK files of an image saved in the five-file DCS (desktop colour separation) format and which is used to preview the image and position it in layouts. Since the composite file is not the one used for separations, you should take care when using it with runaround text. If, for example, you define a path in QuarkXPress, that path will not be contained in the four separation files and the runaround will not work as you planned.

composite video A video 'bus', or signal, in which all the colour information is combined, such as in the 'video out' port on older VCRs (video cassette recorders). This results in loss of quality. On computer monitors, quality is maintained by keeping each of the RGB colour signals separate.

content provider A provider of information on the Web, as distinct from an Internet service provider (ISP).

continuous tone (ct) An image that contains infinite continuous shades between the lightest and darkest tones, as distinct from a line illustration, which has only one shade. Usually used to describe an image before it is either broken up by the dots of a halftone screen for printing or 'dithered' into a pattern of colours for viewing on low-resolution monitors. Also called **contone**.

contrast The degree of difference between adjacent tones in an image (or computer monitor), from the lightest to the darkest. High contrast describes an image with light highlights and dark shadows but with few shades in between, whereas a low-contrast image is one with even tones and few dark areas or highlights.

convergence In colour monitors, the adjustment of the three RGB beams so that they come together in the right place on the screen.

cool colours A subjective term used to describe colours that have a blue or green bias.

cosmetics Sometimes used to describe the overall appearance of an image, such as colour, contrast, sharpness etc.

CRD (Colour Rendering Dictionary) A table that can be downloaded to a PostScript Level II RIP to control PostScript colour handling.

cyan (c) With magenta and yellow, one of the three subtractive primaries and one of the three process colours used in four-colour printing. Sometimes referred to as **process blue**.

cyan printer The plate or film used to print cyan ink in four-colour process printing.

DCS (desktop colour separation) A file format used for outputting image files to colour separation. DCS files combine a low-resolution image for displaying onscreen with high-resolution EPS format data for colour separations. There are two versions of DCS format files: namely DCS 1.0 and DCS 2.0. DCS 1.0 files comprise five files – a single low-resolution composite file for placing in a layout, plus four high-resolution separation files, one each for cyan, magenta, yellow and black. The DCS 2.0 format allows you to save spot colours with the image, which you can choose to save as a single file (thus saving space) or as multiple files, as in DCS 1.0. Clipping paths can also be saved with both DCS 1.0 and DCS 2.0.

DDCP (direct digital colour proof) Any colour proof made directly from digital data without using separation films, such as those produced on an ink-jet printer.

definition The overall quality – or clarity – of an image, determined by the combined subjective effect of graininess (or resolution in a digital image) and sharpness.

degauss(ing) The technique of removing, or neutralizing, any magnetic field that may have built up over time in a colour monitor. Magnetism can distort the fidelity of colour display. Since most modern monitors perform a degauss automatically, this process is usually only necessary on older monitors.

degradability The term applied to Web browsers able to support new advances in HTML technologies while at the same time serving browsers based on previous versions of the technologies.

Delta E (dE) A measurement of colour error or difference based on L*a*b* coordinates.

dense An image that is too dark.

densitometer A precision instrument used to measure the optical density and other properties of colour and light in positive or negative transparencies, printing film, reflection copy, or computer monitors. Also called a **colour coder**. *See* **calibration**.

density The darkness of tone or colour in any image. In a transparency this refers to the amount of light that can pass through it, thus determining the darkness of shadows and the saturation of colour. A printed highlight cannot be any lighter in colour than the colour of the paper it is printed on, while the shadows cannot be any darker than the quality and volume of ink that the printing process will allow.

density range The maximum range of tones in an image, measured as the difference between the maximum and minimum densities (the darkest and lightest tones).

desaturate To reduce the strength or purity of colour in an image, thus making it greyer.

desaturated colour Colour containing a large amount of grey in proportion to the hue.

descreen(ing) The technique of removing a halftone dot pattern from an image to avoid an undesirable moiré pattern occurring when a new halftone screen is applied. This can be achieved in image-editing applications by using built-in filters (effects) to blur the image slightly and then sharpen it. However, you can achieve better results with dedicated image-enhancement applications that do this automatically using sophisticated interpolation methods – you can, for example, choose the amount of descreening according to the quality of printing or the fineness of the halftone, which can cover anything from fine art books to newspapers. *See* **interpolation**.

desktop colour Colour images prepared or generated using a desktop system, where an original is scanned by a desktop scanner, adjusted on a desktop computer, and positioned and output using a page-layout application. The term is often used – not necessarily derogatorily – to indicate colour reproduction of an inferior quality to that produced on a high-end CEPS system.

device-dependent colour Colour space that is specific to a device. A scanner's RGB values are unrelated to a printer's CMYK values for the same colour, because both values depend on the device where the image is generated or from which it is output.

device-independent colour An intermediate colour space to which scanners and printers are calibrated and through which images are translated regardless of what they are prepared or output on.

dichroic filter A filter that permits certain wavelengths of light to pass through, while preventing others.

dichroic fog An aberration in processed film, appearing as a red or green cloud, caused by an imbalance of chemicals in the developer.

diffraction The scattering of light waves as they strike the edge of an opaque surface. In the conventional preparation of halftones, this can affect dot formations.

digital dot A dot generated by a digital computer or device. Digital dots are all the same size whereas halftone dots vary, so, in digitally generated halftones several dots – up to 256 (on a 16 × 16 matrix) – are required to make up each halftone dot.

digital photography The process of either capturing an image with digital equipment or manipulating photographic images on a computer, or both. In both cases, the term describes photographs that are recorded or manipulated in binary form, rather than on film.

digital video interactive (DVI) A computer chip developed by Intel that compresses and decompresses video images.

digitize To convert anything – for example, text, images or sound – into binary form, so that it can be digitally processed, manipulated, stored and reconstructed. In other words, transforming analog to digital.

digitizer Strictly speaking, any hardware device (such as a scanner or camera) that converts drawn or photographed images into binary code, so you can work with them on a computer. However, the term is more commonly used to refer specifically to 'digitizing tablets'.

dither(ing) A technique of interpolation that calculates the average value of adjacent pixels. This technique is used either to add extra pixels to an image – to smooth an edge, for example, as in anti-aliasing – or to reduce the number of colours or greys in an image by replacing them with average values that conform to a predetermined palette of colours. For example, when an image containing millions of colours is converted ('resampled') to a fixed palette ('index') of, say, 256 colours. A colour monitor operating in 8-bit colour mode (256 colours) will automatically create a dithered pattern of pixels. Dithering is also used by some printing devices to simulate colours or tones.

dot A term that can mean one of three things: **(1)** a halftone dot (the basic element of a halftone image), **(2)** a machine dot (the dots produced by a laser printer or imagesetter), or **(3)** a scan dot (strictly speaking, pixels, which comprise a scanned bitmapped image). The three types of dot are differentiated by being expressed in lpi (lines per inch) for a halftone dot, dpi (dots per inch) for a machine dot, and ppi (pixels per inch) for a scan dot – although the latter is sometimes expressed, erroneously, in dpi. Thus, because the term 'dot' is used to describe both halftone and machine dots, scan dots should always be referred to as pixels.

dot/stripe pitch The distance between the dots or pixels (actually, holes or slits in a screen mesh) on your monitor. The closer the dots, the finer the image display – though dot pitch has nothing to do with the resolution of the image itself.

dots per inch (dpi) A unit of measurement used to represent the resolution of devices such as printers and imagesetters; and also (erroneously) of monitors and images, whose resolution should more properly be expressed in pixels per inch (ppi). The closer the dots or pixels (i.e. the more there are to an inch), the better the quality. Typical resolutions are 72ppi for a monitor, 300dpi for a LaserWriter, and 2450dpi (or more) for an imagesetter.

Dynamic HTML/DHTML (Dynamic Hypertext Markup Language) A development of basic HTML code that enables you to add such features as basic animations and highlighted buttons to Web pages without relying on browser plug-ins. DHTML is built into version 4.0 and later-generation Web browsers.

EPS (encapsulated PostScript) A standard graphics file format used primarily for storing object-orientated (or 'vector') graphics files generated by 'drawing applications' such as Adobe Illustrator and Macromedia FreeHand (a vector is a tiny database giving information about both the magnitude and direction of a line or shape). An EPS file usually has two parts: one containing the PostScript code that tells the printer how to print the image, the other an onscreen preview, which can be in PICT, TIFF or JPEG formats. Although used mainly for storing vector-based graphics, the EPS format is also widely used for storing bit-mapped images, particularly those used for desktop colour separation (DCS). Such EPS files are encoded either as ASCII – a text-based description of an image – or in binary, which uses numbers rather than text to store data. Bitmapped EPS files that are to be printed from a Windows-based system use ASCII encoding, whereas ones to be printed on the Mac OS are usually saved with binary encoding, although not all printing software supports binary EPS files.

eyedropper tool In some applications, a tool for gauging the colour of adjacent pixels.

fill In graphics applications, the content, such as colour, tone or pattern, applied to the inside of a closed path or shape, including type characters.

filter (1) Strictly speaking, in computer software a filter can be any component that provides the basic building blocks for processing data. However, the term is more commonly used to describe particular functions within an application (such as importing and exporting data in different file formats) or, in image-editing and drawing applications, those used for applying special effects to images.

filter (2) The coloured-glass, tinted-gelatin or cellulose-acetate sheets used in conventional colour separation that absorb specific wave-lengths of light, so the red, green and blue components of an original can be separated to provide the cyan, magenta, yellow and black films used in process printing.

final rendering The final computer generation of an image, once you have finally finished tweaking and agonizing (in low resolution). For example, application of the final surface texture, lighting and effects to a 3-D object, scene or animation. High-quality renders – particularly of animated scenes – require considerable computer processing power, so banks of linked computers are sometimes used to speed up the process, using a technique called **distributed rendering**.

flat Said of any image – original or printed – that lacks sufficient colour or contrast, for whatever reason.

flat-tint halftone A halftone image printed over a flat tint of colour.

FM screening (frequency modulated screening) A method of screening an image for reproduction that uses a random pattern of dots to reproduce a continuous-tone image. Also known as **stochastic screening**.

FOCOLTONE A colour-matching system in which all of the colours can be created by printing the specified process-colour percentages.

four-colour process Any printing process used to reproduce full-colour images that have been separated into the three basic 'process' colours (cyan, magenta and yellow), with the fourth colour (black) added for extra density.

full colour Synonymous with four-colour reproduction, the term most commonly used to describe process-colour reproduction.

gamma A measure of contrast in a digital image, or in a photographic film or paper, or processing technique.

gamma correction Modification of the mid-tones of an image by compressing or expanding the range, thus altering the contrast. Also known as **tone correction**.

gamut compression Gamut mapping where the range of colour values produced by an input device is compressed to fit into the smaller available gamut of the output device. Gamut compression can be crucial to good colour reproduction, but colours that have been gamut compressed will seldom match the original.

gamut mapping The redistribution of colour values from a colour scanner to fit an output device. If the input gamut is larger than the output gamut, gamut mapping is the same as gamut compression. If the input gamut is smaller then the output gamut, the colours and contrast can be intensified through gamut expansion, or colours can be mapped to their exact equivalents (e.g. for digital proofing).

GCR (grey-component replacement) A colour-separation technique in which black ink is used (instead of overlapping combinations of cyan, magenta and yellow) to create grey shades. This technique avoids colour variations and trapping problems during printing.

GIF *abb.:* **graphic interchange format** A bitmapped graphics format originally devised by Compuserve, an Internet service provider (now part of AOL), and sometimes (although rarely) referred to as Compuserve GIF. There are two specifications: GIF87a and, more recently, GIF89a, the latter providing additional features such as transparent backgrounds. The GIF format uses a lossless compression technique and thus does not squeeze files as much as the JPEG format, which is lossy (some data is discarded). For use in Web browsers, JPEG is the format of choice for tone images such as photographs, whereas GIF is more suitable for line images and other graphics such as text.

Gouraud shading A method, used in 3-D applications, of rendering by manipulating colours and shades selectively along the lines of certain vertices, which are then averaged across each polygon face in order to create a realistic light-and-shade effect.

gradation control A means of adjusting the contrast of specific tonal regions – either equally for all colorants or imaging channels, or separately for independent channels.

graduation/gradation/gradient The smooth transition from one colour/tone to another. The relationship of reproduced lightness

185

values to original lightness values in an imaging process, usually expressed as a **tone curve**.

green One of the three additive colours (red, green, and blue). *See* **additive colours**.

grey Any neutral tone in the range between black and white, with no added colour.

greyscale (1) A tonal scale printed in steps from white to black, used for controlling the quality of both colour and black-and-white photographic processing and also for assessing quality in halftone prints. A greyscale (also called a **step wedge**, **halftone step scale** or **step tablet**) is sometimes printed on the edge of a sheet.

greyscale (2) The rendering of an image in a range of greys from white to black. In a digital image and on a monitor this usually means that an image is rendered with eight bits assigned to each pixel, giving a maximum of 256 levels of grey. Monochrome monitors (used increasingly rarely nowadays) can only display black pixels – in which case, greys are achieved by varying the number and positioning of black pixels using the technique called dithering.

heraldic colours A standard system of representing the basic colours of heraldry by means of monochrome shading, hatching, etc. Used when colour printing is impractical or unwarranted.

high-density In relation to all things digital, a term that invariably means 'more' – and therefore 'better'.

hi-fi colour Any process that increases the colour range of an output imaging device (printer). Refers to extra inks and plates added to the standard CMYK set to improve the colour gamut of offset lithography. The three main hi-fi systems are the Kuppers approach (CMYK + RGB), Pantone®Hexachrome™ (CMYK + orange and green) and MaxCMY (CMYK + extra CMY).

HSL (hue, saturation, lightness) A colour model based upon the light transmitted either in an image or in your monitor – hue being the spectral colour (the actual pigment colour), saturation being the intensity of the colour pigment (without black or white added), and brightness representing the strength of luminance from light to dark (the amount of black or white present). Variously called **HLS** (hue, lightness, saturation), **HSV** (hue, saturation, value), and **HSB** (hue, saturation, brightness).

HTML (Hypertext Markup Language) A text-based page-description language (PDL) used to format documents published on the World Wide Web, and which can be viewed with a Web browser.

http (Hypertext Transfer Protocol) A text-based set of rules by which files on the World Wide Web are transferred, defining the commands that Web browsers use to communicate with Web servers. The vast majority of World Wide Web addresses (URLs) are prefixed with http://.

hue Pure spectral colour, which distinguishes a colour from others. Red is a different hue from blue; and although light red and dark red may contain varying amounts of white or black, they may be the same hue.

ICC (International Colour Consortium) Organization responsible for defining cross-application colour standards.

indeterminate colour A trapping term that describes an area of colour comprising many colours, such as a picture.

indexed colour An image mode of a maximum of 256 colours that is used in some applications, such as Adobe Photoshop, to reduce the file size of RGB images, so they can be used, for example, in multimedia presentations or Web pages. This is achieved by using an indexed table of colours ('a colour look-up table', or CLUT) to which the colours in an image are matched. If a colour in the image does not appear in the table (which can be either an existing table using a known palette of 'safe' colours or one constructed from an image), then the application selects the nearest colour or simulates it by arranging the available colours in a pattern (known as dithering).

interlacing A technique of displaying an image on a Web page in which the image reveals increasing detail as it downloads. Interlacing is usually offered as an option in image-editing applications when saving images in GIF, PNG and progressive JPEG formats.

interpolation A computer calculation used to estimate unknown values that fall between known ones. One use of this process is to re-define pixels in bitmapped images after they have been modified in some way – for instance, when an image is resized (called 'resampling') or rotated, or if colour corrections have been made. In such cases the program makes estimates from the known values of other pixels lying in the same or similar ranges. Interpolation is also used by some scanning and image-manipulation software to enhance the resolution of images that have been scanned at low resolution. Inserting animation values between two keyframes of a movie sequence are also interpolations. Some applications allow you to choose an interpolation method – Photoshop, for example, offers Nearest Neighbor (for fast but imprecise results, which may produce jagged effects), Bilinear (for medium-quality results) and Bicubic (for smooth and precise results, but with slower performance).

inverting A feature of many applications whereby an image bitmap is reversed – so that, for example, the black pixels appear white and vice versa, making a negative image. Inverting also effects colours, turning blue to yellow, green to magenta, and red to cyan. The term 'invert' is sometimes used synonymously (and confusingly) with 'inverse', although the latter is more commonly used to mean reversing a selected area so that it becomes deselected, whilst the deselected area becomes selected.

IT8.7/1 An ISO-standard transmission colour target. CIE data provided with each copy of the target enable scanning devices to be calibrated, characterized or profiled in CIE terms.

IT8.7/2 An independent reflective version of the IT8.7/1 i.e. it has its own CIE data.

JPEG/JPG (Joint Photographic Experts Group) An ISO group that defines compression standards for bitmapped colour images. The abbreviated form (pronounced '*jay-peg*') gives its name to a lossy compressed file format in which the degree of compression from high compression/low quality to low compression/high quality can be defined by the user. This makes the format doubly suitable for images that are to be used either for print reproduction or for transmitting across networks such as the Internet – for viewing in Web browsers, for example. See **lossy compression**.

K, k (key plate) The black printing plate in four-colour process printing, though the name is now more commonly used as shorthand for **process black**. Using the letter K rather than the initial B avoids confusion with blue, even though the abbreviation for process blue is C (cyan). See **CMYK**

Kelvin scale Temperature scale in which 0° is absolute zero. The 'colour temperature' of an object is the temperature a perfectly black radiating object would be if it glowed that shade of colour. Average daylight, for example, is reckoned at 6,500°K for Europe and 5,000°K for North America. Blue colours mean higher temperatures, while reds mean lower temperatures.

knockout An area of background colour that has been masked ('knocked out') by a foreground object, and so does not print. The opposite of 'overprint'.

lap To overlap colours in order to avoid registration problems ('trapping').

layer In some applications and Web pages, a level to which you can consign an element of the design you are working on. Selected layers may be active (meaning you can work on them) or inactive. Some applications may not provide a layering feature but nonetheless may lay items one on top of another in the order that you created them – and in some cases will allow you to send items to the back or bring them to the front.

light table/box A table or box with a translucent glass top lit from below, giving a colour-balanced light suitable for viewing colour transparencies and for colour-matching them to proofs.

lightfast/colourfast Term used to describe ink or other material whose colour is not affected by exposure to artificial or natural light, atmosphere or chemicals.

lightness The tonal measure of a colour relative to a scale running from black to white. Also called 'brightness' or 'value'.

linearization The process of calibrating and compensating a device's inability to see or reproduce a straight line of tones. It is used to ensure that an imagesetter reproduces the same halftone-dot values as the imaging software.

link Mathematical look-up table (LUT) that translates colours from an input device into matching colours on an output device. Changes can be customized in the link to alter or improve the image.

lossless compression Methods of file compression in which no data is lost (as opposed to lossy compression). Both LZW and GIF are lossless-compression formats.

lossy compression Methods of file compression in which some data may be irretrievably lost during compression (as opposed to lossless compression). JPEG is a lossy-compression format.

LZW (Lempel-Ziv-Welch) A widely supported lossless-compression method for bitmapped images. It gives a compression ratio of 2:1 or more, depending on the range of colours in an image (an image that has large areas of flat colour will yield higher compression ratios).

magenta (m) With cyan and yellow, one of the three subtractive primaries, and one of the three process colours used in four-colour printing. Sometimes called **process red**.

mapping In computer parlance, assigning attributes – such as colours – to an image.

matt/matte A flat, slightly dull surface.

mean noon sunlight An arbitrary colour temperature to which most daylight colour films are balanced, based on the average colour temperature of direct sunlight at midday in Washington, DC (5,400°K).

median filter A filter in some image-editing applications that removes small details by replacing a pixel with an averaged value of its surrounding pixels, ignoring extreme values.

metameric A colour that changes hue under different lighting conditions.

midtones/middletones The range of tonal values in an image anywhere between the darkest and lightest – usually referring to those approximately halfway.

mode change Transformation of an image from one mode to another.

model Any control specification used for comparing the behaviour of complex systems – a colour model, for example.

monitor Your computer screen, or the unit that houses it. Variously referred to as screens, displays, VDUs and VDTs, monitors display images in colour, greyscale or monochrome, and are available in a variety of sizes (which are measured diagonally), ranging from 9in (229mm) to 21in (534mm) or more. Although most monitors use cathode-ray tubes, some contain liquid-crystal displays (LCDs), particularly portables and laptops and, more recently, gas plasma (large matrices of tiny, gas-filled glass cells).

mono(chrome)/monochromatic Term used to describe an image of varying tones reproduced in a single colour.

monochrome monitor A computer monitor that displays pixels as either black or white – rather than in shades of grey, as on a grey-scale monitor.

monotone Reproduction in a single colour, without tonal variation.

MPEG (Motion Picture Experts Group) A compression format for squeezing full-screen VHS-quality digital video files and animations, providing huge compression ratios – of up to 200:1.

Munsell notation Colour-ordering system specifying the three qualities/attributes: hue, value and chroma. Expressed as H V/C.

noise function A random-pattern generator for rendering colours in 3-D scenes – thus improving photorealism.

output target Series of colour samples of the range of output-device colorant combinations. An output profile is created by putting the resulting CIE values in a table together with the colorant combinations that produced them.

PAL (phase alternation by line) Colour-television system prevalent in most of Western Europe (but not in France). It uses 625 lines and displays images at 25 frames per second.

187

PANTONE® The registered trademark of Pantone Inc.'s system of colour standards and control and quality requirements, in which each colour bears a description of its formulation (in percentages) for subsequent printing. The PANTONE MATCHING SYSTEM® is used throughout the world – consequently colours specified by any designer can be matched exactly by any printer.

pastel shades Shades of colour that are generally both lighter and less saturated than their equivalent bright hue.

patch A single sample.

PPD (PostScript Printer Description) A file describing the features and capabilities of a PostScript printer.

PEL (picture element) The smallest unit of a computer display that can be assigned an individual colour and intensity (usually a pixel).

Phong shading A superior but time-consuming method of rendering 3-D images that computes the shading of every pixel. Usually used for final 32-bit renders.

PICS animation Macintosh animation format that uses PICT images to create a sequence.

PICT A standard file format for storing bit-mapped and object-oriented images on Macintosh computers. Originally, the PICT format only supported eight colours, but a newer version, PICT2, supports 32-bit colour.

pigment Particles of ground colour, dissolved in a suitable medium to form ink or paint.

pixel Acronym for 'picture element'. The smallest component of a digitally generated image, such as a single dot of light on a computer monitor. In its simplest form, one pixel corresponds to a single bit: 0 = off (white) and 1 = on (black). In colour and greyscale images or monitors, a single pixel may correspond to several bits: an 8-bit pixel, for example, can be displayed in any of 256 colours (the total number of different configurations that can be achieved by eight 0s and 1s).

pixel depth The number of shades that a single pixel can display, determined by the number of bits used to display the pixel. One bit equals a single colour (black); four bits (any permutation of four 1s and 0s, such as 0011

or 1001) produces 16 shades; and so on, up to 32 bits (although actually only 24 – the other eight being reserved for functions such as masking), which produces 16.7 million colours.

plug-ins A third-party filter or subprogram that supplements a host application.

PNG (portable network graphics) A file format for images used on the Web that provides 10 to 30 per cent lossless compression, and supports variable transparency through alpha channels, cross-platform control of image brightness, and interlacing.

posterize/posterization To divide, by photographic or digital means, a continuous-tone image into either a predefined or arbitrary number of flat tones. Also known as **tone separation**.

PostScript Page-description language. PostScript code tells an output device how to construct page elements.

primary colours Pure colours from which theoretically (though not in practice) all other colours can be mixed. In printing, they are the 'subtractive' pigment primaries (cyan, magenta and yellow). The primary colours of light, or 'additive' primaries, are red, green and blue.

profile The colorimetric description of an input or output device.

progressive JPEG A digital-image format used for displaying JPEG images on Web pages. The image is displayed in progressively increasing resolutions as the data is downloaded to the browser. Also called **proJPEG**.

purity The degree of saturation of a colour.

red One of the three additive primary colours (red, green and blue).

reference colours Colours that are familiar to most people and thus easy to remember, such as sky blue, grass green, etc.

registration colour In many graphics applications, a default colour that, when applied to items such as crop marks, will print on every separation plate.

relative colorimetry Values are relative to the white point of the device or image, rather than absolute CIE values.

relative densitometry Densities calculated by subtraction from the white point of the image or device. Relative reflection densities are calculated relative to white paper density. Relative transmission densities are calculated relative to the clear film base.

RGB (red, green, blue) The primary colours of the 'additive' colour model – used in video technology (including computer monitors) and also for graphics (for the Web and multimedia, for example) that will not ultimately be printed by the four-colour (CMYK) process method.

RIP (Raster Imaging Processor) A device that converts page-description data (e.g. PostScript) into a form for output to an imagesetter.

sampling/sample A measurement of data – such as a pixel – averaged across a small 'snapshot' of that data in order to make modifications. For example, assessing the density of shadows in an image by taking a sample across a few pixels with an appropriate tool (usually an 'eyedropper').

saturation The variation in colour of the same tonal brightness from none (grey), through pastel shades (low saturation), to pure colour with no grey (high saturation, or 'fully saturated'). Also called 'purity' or 'chroma'.

screen angle The angle at which halftone screens of images printing in two or more colours are positioned to minimize undesirable dot patterns (moiré) when printed. The angle at which screens should be positioned depends upon the number of colours being printed, but the normal angles for four-colour process printing are: cyan 105°, magenta 75°, yellow 90°, black 45°.

screen capture A 'snapshot' of part or all of a monitor display. Also called a 'screen shot', 'screen grab' or 'screen dump'.

screen frequency The number of line rulings per inch (lpi) on a halftone screen.

separation filters The filters used to separate colours so that they can be printed individually. They each transmit about one-third of the spectrum.

separation guide A printed guide containing a set of standard colours (such as cyan, magenta, yellow, red, green, blue and black) which, when photographed alongside a colour-critical subject (a painting, for example), allow the separation to be matched against the colour-control bar printed alongside the image.

sepia A brown colour, and also a monochrome print in which the normal shades of grey appear as shades of brown.

shading In 3-D applications, the resulting colour of a surface due to light striking it at an angle.

shadow areas The areas of an image that are darkest or densest.

sharpening Enhancing the apparent sharpness of an image by increasing the contrast between adjacent pixels.

smoothing The refinement of bitmapped images and text by a technique called 'anti-aliasing' (adding pixels of an 'in-between' tone). Smoothing is also used in some drawing and 3-D applications, where it is applied to a path to smooth a line, or to 'polygons' to tweak resolution in the final render.

spectrophotometer Device for measuring luminous energy at various frequencies throughout the spectrum. Spectral data can be displayed as CMY density, L*a*b* or XYZ.

spectrum Series of colours that results when normal white light is dispersed into its component parts by refraction through a prism.

specular map In 3-D applications, a texture map – such as those created by noise filters – that is used instead of specular colour to control highlights.

specular reflectance The reflection (as by a mirror) of light rays at an angle equal to the angle at which it strikes a surface (angle of incidence).

subtractive colours The colour model describing the primary colours of reflected light: cyan, magenta, and yellow (CMY). Subtractive colours form the basis for printed process colours.

SuperVGA (SVGA) A video display standard that supports 256 colours or more in a variety of resolutions.

surface In 3-D applications, the matrix of control points and line end points underlying a mapped texture or colour.

swatch A colour sample.

SWOP (Specifications for Web Offset Publications) A system of standards developed for the printing industry to aid consistency in the use of colour-separation films and colour proofing.

taper Referring to graduated tones and colours, the progression of one tone or colour to the next.

taper angle The direction in which graduated tones or colours merge into one another.

Targa A digital-image format for 24-bit image files, commonly used by computer systems in the MS-DOS environment that contain the Truevision video board.

tertiary colour The resulting colour when two secondary colours are mixed.

TIFF, TIF (tagged image file format) A standard and popular graphics file format – originally developed by Aldus (now merged with Adobe) and Microsoft – that is used for scanned high-resolution bitmapped images, and for colour separations. The TIFF format can be used for black-and-white, greyscale and colour images that have been generated on different computer platforms.

tint The resulting shade when white is added to a solid colour.

tint sheet A preprinted sheet of halftone tints, patterns and other designs that are cut and pasted onto camera-ready artwork.

tonal value/tone value The relative densities of tones in an image.

transparent GIF A feature of the GIF89a file format that allows you to place a non-rectangular image on the background colour of a Web page.

trichromatic Comprising three colours.

tristimulus values The amounts of red, green and blue light of specific bandwidths and wavelengths needed for a certain colour.

tritone A halftone image that is printed using three colours. Typically, a black-and-white

image is enhanced by the addition of two colours. For example, when added to black, process yellow and magenta will produce a sepia-coloured image.

TRUMATCH colours A system of colour matching used for specifying process colours.

unsharp masking (USM) A traditional film-compositing technique used to 'sharpen' an image. This can also be achieved digitally – by means of image-editing applications that use filters to enhance the details in a scanned image by increasing the contrast of pixels (the exact amount depending on various criteria such as the 'threshold' specified and the radius of the area around each pixel).

unwanted colours Three colour patches on colour reproduction guides that record the same as the white patch when separated. For example, the blue, cyan and magenta patches on a yellow separation record the same as the white patch.

wanted colours Three colour patches on colour reproduction guides that record the same as the black patch when separated. For example, the yellow, red and green patches on a yellow separation record the same as the black patch.

warm colours Any colour with a hue veering towards red or yellow – as opposed to cool colours, which veer towards blue or green.

white light The colour of light resulting from red, blue and green being combined in equal proportions.

yellow (y) With cyan and magenta, one of the three subtractive primaries, and one of the three process colours used in four-colour printing. Sometimes called **process yellow**.

189

INDEX

URLs